TABOO
NO
MORE

TABOO
NO
MORE

The Phallus in Fact, Fiction and Fantasy

HONI
SOIT
QUI
MAL
Y
PENSE

DR. MARK THORN

Foreword by
Ashley Montagu

NEW YORK

SHAPOLSKY PUBLISHERS

9 8 7 6 5 4 3 2 1

Library of Congress Catalog Card Number 89-061991
ISBN 0-944007-63-5

Book designed by Karin Kincheloe.

Manufactured by Tradeglobe, (H.K.) Ltd.

Typeset by Village Type & Graphics, New York

Distributed by the Carol Publishing Group

To my wife,
my love

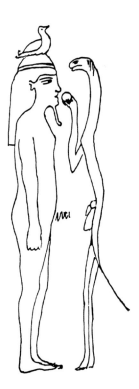

● Ancient carving discovered in
Egypt, depicts the story of the
forbidden fruit and of primige-
nial carnal knowledge as told
in the Bible and in other scriptures of past civilizations.

FOREWORD

*T*he 9th century was remarkable for, among other things, the number of books and treatises on what was called "Phallic Worship." The truth is that there never was such a thing as "phallic worship," and while in legend and ritual the penis was celebrated, it never formed a dominant motif or totality of any known religion. It might figure in art, or in ritual head dress, as in some Hopi Kachinas, but it was seldom if ever in any prurient sense. Nonetheless, the chronic male preoccupation with sex has, in every patriarchal society—and in almost every known society the dominant sex has been male, and as the author writes in this intriguing book, "Man's sexuality, voluptuousness, and salaciousness, as well as his transcendent longings, are triggered by the penis." It is, therefore, to be expected that wherever the facts have yielded to inquiry or observation, the penis, in one form or another, has played a prominent role in the life of virtually every society. It is to this that Dr. Thorn has devoted his attention in the pages of this book. He has read widely and well, and if he has not burdened his pages with footnotes, he has written an engaging and highly readable account of one of the most widely distributed, but seldom openly acknowledged, major preoccupations of man.

Princeton, New Jersey
Ashley Montagu

INTRODUCTION

*W*hatever else this book might be, it is neither a historical
study of phallus worship nor a probe into human biology.
It is rather a mélange of thoughts and reveries centering on
the facts and myths about the sexual aspect of human existence,
thoughts flowing from an open mind and seeking anagogical
meaning. In essence, this work offers a personal view of the role of
the phallus IN RELIGION AND RITUAL WORSHIP, IN ART
AND ARTIFACTS, IN HEDONISM AND DEBAUCHERY,
IN POLITICS AND SATIRE.

Dedicated to the free man of conscience striving to reconcile spirit
and flesh, the infinite in him with his mortal body. Said Kierkegaard:
"Had spirit not breathed forth synthesis of soul and body, sexuality
as we know it would never have made its entry into the world."

ODE TAE A PENIS
by Robert Burns*

Puir wee soft and flabby penis,
A wheen o' pleasure ye hae gien us.
An hour or twa ago, puir thing,
Ye made my lassie's gled hert sing,
For ye struck oot sae firm and prood
An' put Jean Armour in the mood.

She doted with the love ye gied,
An' lost wi' glee her maidenheid.
But noo, puir thing, ye look sae sad,
You're no use noo tae Rabbie lad.

And as I slowly puff my pipe
You look just like some wrinkled tripe.
But still ye did a guid night's work;
Ye did your duty, and didnae shirk.
She lay there, gigg'lin wi' pleasure;
Lie doon, and rest—ye've earned your leisure.

You're wabbit oot, an' soft as butter—
But think hoo ye made Jeannie splatter.
Ye squirmed just like a tremblin' jelly,
As ye went scuddin' up her belly.

Her comely thighs, her arse sae braw
    Did answer nature's ca'.
Fu' prood Ah wis o' hard-worked penis:
O' coorse ye jerked there weel atween us;
Ye gied yer a' tae satisfy
The urgent need o' Jean and I.

But noo my bonnie Jean's gane hame
Tae hing her head in sorry shame.
Ye ken best whit ye did her wrang—
Ah kept ye in for far too lang,
An noo I'll hae tae wait an' see
If Jean will hae her pregnancy.

Oh weel, we a' maun tak oor chances,
Let's saunter doon tae Poosie Nansy's,
An' when I've had a dram or twa
I'll let you pish again' the wa'.
Ye'll maybe pardon my abuses
An' realize ye've ither uses.

*Attributed to.

1.

Legend came first, knowledge later. "Man is eager after knowledge, and the love of legend is but the prelude of it," said the ancient Greek historian Strabo. It has been said that when God, in His infinite wisdom and grand configuration, conceived man, He, the Master Potter, started with the penis, which turned out to be the most imaginative and fascinating organ of the human body, possibly the most tantalizing protoplast in the universe, the life force itself. Thus, when the Master molded the animal kingdom, He gave it a master-key to perpetuate life in the whole macrocosm.

The mythmakers of antiquity considered the penis to be a separate living entity, apart from the human body, and treated it as a divinity of celestial origin. In all languages, primitive or advanced, the penis has been referred to in the masculine gender, as "he," rather than in the neuter, as "it."

Flaccid or erect, circumcised or uncircumcised, the penis has an intriguing shape. While being metaphoric as no other part of the human body, he is the most functional and cogent tool ever conceived. He is tangible and yet intangible, a fact and yet a myth. While he is a sublime and irresistible attraction, he has a life and a will of his own and a brain whose processes elude perception. Shakespeare, puzzling over this phenomenon, wrote: "How strange it is that desire outlasts performance."

The penis affects our dreams and is a key to the inner self. He tries to express the inexpressible through the act of penetration, as if reaching for infinite mystical divinity. More sensitive to the touch than any other part of the body, the penis is not subject to volition; he acts and reacts in his own unpredictable way. This is probably why even primitive man covered that part of his naked body when roaming the wilds. The penis's reaction to hunger is unlike that of any living thing on earth. The Talmud says: "There is a small member of the human body; when it is starved, it is satiated; when it is fed, it is hungry." To put it in contemporary parlance, "Use it or

• Cameo and seal of Messalina and Claudius (first century A.D.).

lose it!" He can be asleep when we are wide awake, he can be awake when we are fast asleep. He is the only segment of the body absolutely defiant of mind over matter. He can say yes when we say no and say no or maybe when we say yes. He is emotional, sensitive to kisses, to caresses, to rudeness, to overwork. He has a sense of beauty and smell. He can conceptualize thoughts. He is self-conscious in his own way and in his own time, and yet has no inferiority complex. He gets insulted and in turn can be insulting. He can be indignant and can be humiliating. He can smile and laugh, and can cry tears unabashedly. He is coy and timid when flaccid, but ferocious, bold, and relentless when provoked. He can be most beastly and cruel, sighting his prey from afar and scheming his own assault. The only tumescent portion of the body, the penis expands quixotically to several times his dormant size, to reach out for pleasurable sensations, and in the process becomes the most powerful key to human needs.

Man's sensuality, voluptuousness, and salaciousness, as well as his transcendent longings, are triggered by the penis. A highly charged magnet, the penis ultimately controls our gratification or frustration, our exhilaration or delusion. His ejaculation and sperm are nothing if not a sublime expression of his anagogical existence.

While other parts of the body—such as limbs, skin, and hair—have undergone substantial changes over the course of human evolution, the penis has most likely remained the same since the Paleolithic Age. He also is the only part of the human body not directly controlled by the mind in the same way that the limbs and fingers are. In fact, there can be no completely passionate coitus unless the noetic state can be escaped from and the mind can be switched off.

Of all the animals on Earth, none is as oblivious to his own consciousness as man is when seeking the delirium of coitus. The

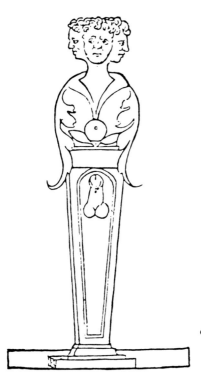

- **Vignette from the novel
Poliphilo (Francesco Colonna),
15th century.**

more the penis is aroused, the more a man relinquishes his *penetralia mentis* and the equilibrium of his rational mind—so much so that his reason and logic are entirely subdued at the height of the climax, the ultimate fusion of the sensual with the spiritual, often followed by a slump into desolation.

In *Antigone*, Sophocles says "Whoever touches you is at once thrown into delirium." And Shakespeare, in "A Lover's Complaint," puts it thus: "Love's arms are peace 'gainst rule, 'gainst sense, 'gainst shame." Homer sees the penis as a corruptor of man's will, and the climax as "the sweet bewitching moods which steal the wits from the wisest man." Socrates describes man's sexual urge as the "sting of a tarantula." Montaigne refers to the penis as a sleepy animal whose awakening gets more difficult with age. Robert Burns, who wrote paeans to, and bestowed lavish praise on, his penis, calls the male organ a mediator and peace-maker, "the umpire,

the bond of union, the pleni-potentiary, the Aaron's rod, the Ahasuerus's sceptre, the sword of mercy, the philosopher's stone, the horn of plenty, the Tree of Life."

The contemporary Israeli author Amos Oz, in his *A Perfect Peace*, compares the penis to "the cane of a furious blind man."

Isaac Bashevis Singer avers that "The sexual organs are the most sensitive organs of the human being. The eye or the ear seldom sabotage you. An eye will not stop seeing if it doesn't like what it sees, but the penis will stop functioning if he doesn't like what he sees. I would say that the sexual organs express the human soul more than any other limb of the body."

The arcane spell that traps a man and renders him all-oblivious when he is aroused by the sexual wiles of the female is best expressed by Charles Baudelaire in "Metamorphoses of the Vampire":

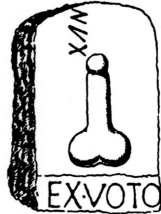

Roman carving on stone. Inscription reads: "Ex voto" ("With a Vow").

~

All sorrows die upon my bosom. I can make
Old men laugh happily as children for my sake.
For him who sees me naked in my tresses, I
Replace the sun, the moon, and all the stars of the sky!
Believe me, learned sir, I am so in voluptuary skilled
That when I smother a lover in my soft arms, and yield
My breasts like two ripe fruits for his devouring—both
Timid and libertine, fragile and robust—
Upon this bed that groans, sighs, and swoons
Even the impotent angels would be damned for me!

~

Although the perplexity of *non compos mentis* is unique to the human species, the animal kingdom is not completely lacking in delirium during copulation. It is said that, when in coitus, the omnivorous raven has tears in his eyes and that the orthopterous preying mantis devours his offspring when copulating.

2. _____

It is conceivable that before he transgressed and ate from the Tree of Knowledge, the first hominid had a protoplastic composition identical to that of the penis of present-day man. One might argue that the entire human body once consisted of the same flabby substance as that of the male organ of today—where chemistry and mass, consciousness and the senses were merged, creating a state of trance. Transcendental meditation, yoga, and all other forms of physical or mental discipline are no more than desperate attempts by man to resurrect artificially that state of languor. The deep sleep that God caused upon Adam was probably also caused upon Eve when she, too, acquired the knowledge of good and evil. The Lord's admonition to Adam against eating the fruit of knowledge, under penalty of death, was only a metaphoric caution against transmutation. The sly serpent understood it well when he beguiled Eve, saying, "Ye shall not surely die." And he was right. The serpent, it seems, was a higher organism which had achieved conceptual thought before our ancestors did. (The Gnostics, a hybrid religious faction of early Christians combining Christianity with Oriental thought, perceived the snake as a symbol of intellect.)

In the Garden of Eden, the serpent gave Eve knowledge of the penis—a phenomenon which over the millennia has repeatedly generated inspiration in art, science, and poetry while nourishing female discontent, envy, and perfidy and thus establishing forever the cunning reptile as the analogue of the male organ. The Lord "put enmity between the serpent and the woman, and his seed and her seed." This marked the beginning of the love-hate relationship whose dichotomy becomes almost graphic in Synthia, the moon goddess fabled to have been a beautiful woman from the buttocks up and a viper in her lower part.

Having the power to erect himself like a penis and to shed his skin, presumably thereby renewing his youth, the snake, in varying postures, also became the symbol of health, vigor, and desire, and as such was represented by ancient peoples as a mythological deity: sometimes wreathed around fertile eggs, at other times with his tail in the mouth—the tail forming a ring—to suggest wisdom and eternity in the mystical order of the universe. In the latter position, the snake as a symbol is used by the Theosophic Society for its seal. When the serpent twines around a rod, it stands for the erect organ under the spell of sexual passion. It is in this configuration that the serpent appears on the staff originally held by Christian bishops and called the staff of life. In some primitive languages, the word for serpent is the same as that for life.

In the groves of Aesculapius, the Greek and Roman god of medicine, snakes were kept exclusively for prophecies. A naked virgin carrying food would be sent into the groves, and the reaction of the snakes to her appearance would foretell a good or a bad future. Milk-fed snakes were used in the same way for prognosis of sick patients who came to the temple to consult the oracles. The extent of an illness was determined in clinics set up in the temple. Young, specially trained girls would mingle with male patients and test the men's vigor in a sexual encounter. The weak and apathetic were considered far-gone in their disease.

The penis pursues his own growth and maturity. He manifests one of the first signs of body sensation; he becomes alive and erect when we are still babies; in fact, some believe that erection can occur even in the fetus. His length and circumference are independent of body size. His life span is unpredictable and his aging process unnoticeable. He never looks young or old throughout his existence. At his own choosing, he can go into hibernation for his lifetime, and if we believe in phenomenalism, he can occasionally erect himself after we die. To be sure, the penis conjures man more often than man conjures the penis. In fact, the penis understands himself better than man understands man. In our days, the film *Deep Throat*—its pornographic aims notwithstanding—came the closest to expressing the baffling nature of the penis and his need for love and compassion.

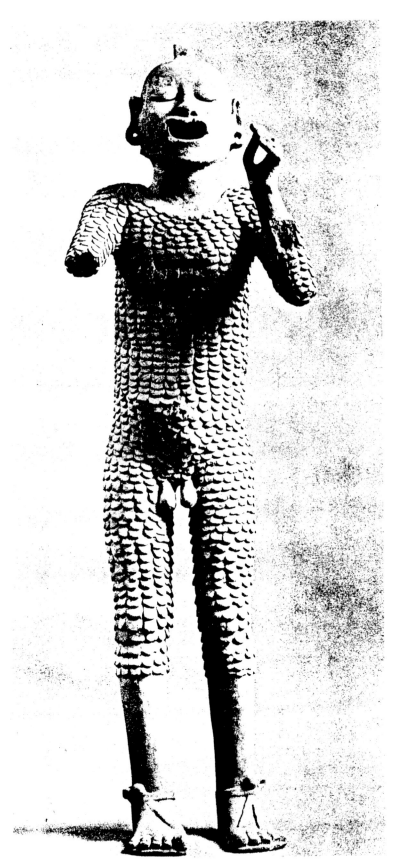

- XIP TOTE (God of Growth and Rejuvenation), Aztec Civilization (1300-1520), Central Mexico. The one-piece suit with scales represents the skin of a sacrificial human. The slit in the chest shows where the victim's heart was removed.

● Japanese phallic object, colored stone with Buddhist cross. Adapted by the Nazis as their emblem and referred to as the Swastika. (18th century A.D.)

In his longing for eternal youth, man secretly dreams of a lifelong waking sensuality and of vigor, represented by the ability to sustain an erection at will, without which a zestful life seems waning. In his *Unfinished Business*, John Houseman (1902-1988) talks about the passage of years and of some acquaintances for whom "at [the age of] 60 the threats of impotence and enforced retirement present rich opportunities for apprehension and gloom." No doubt, whether awake or dreaming, man has an enigmatic relationship with his penis. Every man's state of mind and body depends upon the degree of harmony or conflict between himself and his penis.

Thus, consciously or unconsciously, the penis is the very center of human life: Love, sex, passion, lust, procreation, offspring—all these and more—pass through his amazing urge or the absence of it. Man's moods, his happiness or depression—and eventually his destiny—are all determined by the penis, which in turn is mysteriously linked to the infinite and the eternal. To borrow Plato's phrase used in another context, all things arise from it, and into it all things resolve.

No wonder that recently medical researchers took a closer look at man's impotence and its traumatic effects on millions of people. It is estimated that one out of ten males in the United States agonizes secretly over erection disorders, a condition which has long been thought to be only psychological. Today medical science has established that a sustained erection is the result of a combination of neurological, sensory and psychological stimuli. A breakthrough is now in progress to overcome the pathology of impotence, both by drugs and by prostheses. In the first instance, a drug is injected directly into the penis, in the second instance, the treatment may consist of a sleeve with low electric current called MEGS (Male Electronic Genital Stimulator) which is applied trans-rectally. It is estimated that more than 100,000 men in the United States are hooked up with such a prosthesis. Another method is penile implant surgery.

Pablo Ruiz Picasso (1881-1973).
"Drawing for Crucifixion" (1929).
Metaphoric reshuffling of
female anatomy that may appear
as either mouth or vulva, nose
or penis, breast or testicles.

Cameos made of semiprecious stones and gold, used in the Middle Ages as amulets against infertility.

Male impotence no longer is the taboo that it once was. Some communities in the United States have formed I.A. (Impotents Anonymous)—patterned after A.A. (Alcoholics Anonymous)—where men and their partners talk freely about the problem of impotence.

The sun—given its effect on the senses and its power to regenerate all living matter in Nature—became the image of masculinity sustaining all life on Earth. Deeply rooted in prehistory, this symbol of masculinity was called *phallós* (phallus) by the Greeks, was deified, and emerged as the compendious icon of the masses. And from the deification of such phallic symbols grew out all other religions and civilizations.

Jewish Scriptures hold that nothing but the mind is the source of human existence, and so they damn evil thoughts because thoughts can find their way into the body itself. Spinoza, too, considers a free man one whose inner awareness of oneself and of Nature is guided by reason or intuition rather than by desire and the senses. Yet the early Greeks viewed human emotion, desire, and ideas as springing from the generative organ. Later, Gnostic doctrine made it the prime duty of every man to follow his instinct and yearning. Schopenhauer, too, claims that man's philosophies are built around his desires; and Freud and Kinsey refined the theory in contemporary terms. Freud assumes, and in a way Kinsey confirms, that the energy source of human behavior is to be found largely in the sexual impulse even as man's very character and personality dynamics depend upon the degree of his libido.

3.

To the ancient cosmogonists, the first stage of life after the reign of chaos was androgynous. Animation came with the injection into the cosmos of the ethereal essence of the Creator. Was the Creator Himself androgynous? God Himself has the privilege to be man or woman, or both. He obviously chose to be both. "In the day that God created man, in the likeness of God made He them; and God blessed them and called their name Adam," says the Bible. Adam, the progenitor of the human race, was thus androgynous and, by possessing the organs of both sexes, produced offspring of each. According to Philo Judaeus, a contemporary of Jesus, Adam was a double being, or a hermaphrodite, in the likeness of God. Says Philo: "God seperated Adam into his two sexual component parts, one male, the other female. The longing for reunion, which love inspired in the divided halves of the original bisexual being, is the source of sexual pleasure, which is the beginning of all transgression."

It is fabled that while Zeus was asleep, he had a nocturnal emission and dropped his seed on the earth. From this seed grew a demon with both male and female genitals. Plato also asserts that the human species was androgynous before Zeus separated it in two halves which forever seek to be reunited. Others speculate that early woman was an imperfect male who lost his male parts in the process of evolution. And Andreas Vesalius, a sixteenth-century Flemish anatomist, suggests that women possess all the basic male elements, except that these elements are interfused within the female body—a theory similar to that advanced by Sigmund Freud centuries later.

The Talmud, too, makes reference to the androgynous state of the first man conceived as male in his right side and as female in his left. In fact, in the mysticism of the Kabbalah, the right side of every living body is considered to be male, the left female. Jewish Scriptures, however, also divide man's body horizontally; an expurgated upper half and an ever-unclean lower part. Up to this day orthodox Jews wear a special belt during prayer, to emphasize the difference between the two halves.

• **Vladimir Malakhov and Valeria Tosoi as Adam and Eve in the Moscow Classical Ballet's production of "The Creation of the World," 1988. Serpent-worship, or ophiolatry, glorifies the generative powers of the serpent and is associated with the Original Sin.**

Much like the Bible, which—in modern interpretation—portrays Adam as predominatly male and Eve as having been metagenetically fashioned from his rib, the Hindu Purama suggests that the first man's left side came as a byproduct of his right male side. To the ancient Greeks, on the other hand, woman was a punishment sent to Earth by Zeus in the guise of Pandora, whose only dowry for her husband-to-be, Epimetheus, consisted of a box filled with all the ills and sorrows of life.

Thus, in both religion and mythology, as much biologically as spiritually, woman at once participates in the genesis of man and owes her own genesis to man; when all is said and done, woman is a part of man. Coitus actually is an expression of the craving for reunification of the two divided parts. It is an act of coalescence which merges at once the spirit and the body of the two sexes with one another.

Whatever the effects and ramifications of the unisex movement of today may turn out to be, fulfillment of the natural desire for copulation and woman's urge to procreate—in evidence since the dawn of time—will to the end remain subject only to the will of the male. The vagina will perpetually seek out man, without whose erect penis intercourse cannot be achieved and the species cannot survive. The act of male ejaculation is essential to fertilization, whereas sexual orgasm in the female is not. "Your desire shall be to your husband, and he shall rule over you," exhorted the Lord God. The conception of active and passive, and the precept that the passive must accomodate itself to the active are a direct corollary of the Biblical exhortation. Man first, woman second: not equal.

John Milton, in *Paradise Lost,* poetizes the conjugation of Adam and Eve:

> The image of their glorious maker shone,
> Truth, wisdom, sanctitude severe and pure,
> Severe but in true filial freedom placed;
> Whence true authority in men; though both
> Not equal, as their sex not equal seemed;
> For contemplation he and valor formed,
> For softness she and sweet attractive grace.
> He for God only, she for God in him.

Henri de Toulouse-Lautrec, French artist (1864-1901). Titled "Soleil Couchant" (Sunset).

Henri de Toulouse-Lautrec (1864-1901), French artist. Titled "Sportive."

Walt Whitman, obviously reacting to the male's attitude toward women at that time, stated in *Four Poems from Song of Myself:* "I say it is as great to be a woman as to be a man."

The Jewish male, in his daily prayer, thanks God that He did not make him a woman. In the same prayer, women thank the Lord for making them according to His desire. The Gnostics saw salvation for women only in metamorphosis. Their Gospel says: "Every woman who will make herself male will enter the Kingdom of Heaven."

The perception of an existing chasm between the male and the female of the species has pervaded the thinking of both philosophical and religious minds. In his *Politics*, Aristotle says that ". . . the male is by nature superior, and the female inferior; and the one rules, and the other is ruled; this principle, of necessity, extends to all mankind . . . . The courage of a man is shown in commanding, of a woman in obeying." St. Augustine says: "A husband is meant to rule over his wife as the spirit rules the flesh."

Even the Virgin Mary—by virtue of being a woman and, therefore, the passive element in the coming of the Son of God—was thought by early Christians to be inferior in sanctity and dignity to the Apostles. When the Apostles spread out to preach the Gospel, they carried no crucifix and had no reverence for the Virgin Mary (nor was the doctrine of the Trinity known to them, for that matter). Throughout evolution, the egg, by its very nature, has been the passive element, and the sperm, the active element. The ancient Ammonites called the active and passive powers of Nature "male" and "female." Jewish religious doctrine defines the two sexes as "bestower" and "bestowee."

4. _____

*L*egend has it that when Adam first became conscious of his nudity, he covered his genitals with a fig leaf. He also put a leaf on Eve. Actually, there was nothing on her to cover. He did it only out of galantry. This might have been the first gentlemanly act of the human species which has come down to us, among other male-to-female courtesies, as today's helping a woman with her coat. The fig itself became the symbol of what Adam covered with his leaf; the fig leaf, because of its shape, became the symbol of the male triade; and the fig tree, as it generally yields fruit all year round, became the symbol of procreation, and was sacred to the god Bacchus. Could it be that the long history of indulgence of women by men is rooted in the male's compassion for the female's not possessing a penis?

When confronted with the male, the female is pervaded by a deep sense of inadequacy. It is not unusual for little girls to ask, disappointed, why they do not have the same thing as the boys.

The seventh-century B.C. poet Semonides of Amorgos ungallantly compared women to "foxes, asses, and a changeful sea," swearing that no husband has ever lived through a day without some word of censure from his wife. Tennyson, in "Locksley Hall," says: "Woman is the lesser man, and all thy passions, watched with mine,/ Are as moonlight unto sunlight, and water unto wine." Strindberg, for his part, gave vent to his misogyny when he posited: "Women being small and foolish and therefore evil . . . should be suppressed like barbarians and thieves. She is useful only as ovary and womb." Another Swede, a philosopher and an authority on art, Karl August Ehrensvad, wrote: "There are two things I shall never cease to believe, firstly, that woman's freedom destroys man's way of thinking, and secondly, that the equality in which we live causes a pursuit of happiness which impoverishes all of us."

One need not question the tenets of women's liberation to recognize that a convex is different from a concave and that

• **Attributed to the French humanist and satirist François Rabelais (1494-1553). Phallic caricature of a syphilitic Pope Julius II (1443-1513).**

the inherent property of the bolt is not the same as that of the nut. Perfervid women who accuse men of despotism do not understand that manhood is not a rational, but a biological, state of being. By nature man is master in any situation or position of coitus, no matter how contentious the woman may be. He makes love to her, not she to him. The *Homo sapiens,* more than any other animal, is biologically programmed for male dominance. Man feels dominant (often mistaken for superior) because of the very nature of his crypto-chemical composition which gets its electrical impulses from the penis, the center of man's physical and emotional existence.

By claiming that "penetration was never meant to be kind" and that "coitus is punishment," Andrea Dworkin, in *Intercourse* (much as Catharine MacKinnon, in *Feminism Unmodified*), seems to attribute the male's sexual dominance to a state of mind. Scientists, however, don't see male supremacy as a state of mind. They speculate that the consummation of the sexual act between male and female is contingent

upon the level of serotonin, one of the neurotransmitters that control the activity of brain cells. The level of serotonin presumably rises in the male when he is in body contact with the female, thus increasing the male dominance factor, whereas in the female the level of serotonin decreases considerably—her only natural way of self-realization. Neuroanatomists have already established differences in the structure of male and female human brains. Studies in animals clearly indicate that such differences exist.

And with or without equal-rights amendments to the American Constitution, with or without unisex fads, with or without mixed contact sports, the battle of the sexes as dominant and submissive will go on forever. The male will inherently continue to be overriding as *primus inter pares,* and sexism will prevail. This is because deep in the innermost recesses of woman's subconscious, her very lack of penis will remain eternally the source of her envy of the cooing male who possesses the precious organ she lacks. Freud speaks of inferiority of the

• Attributed to the French
humanist and satirist François
Rabelais (1494-1553). A phallic
caricature of the French King
François I (1494-1547).

clitoris vis-a-vis the penis, and "the female
dominated by penis-envy." Darwin himself,
in his vision of the evolution of the species,
stated: "Man has ultimately become
superior to woman" (*The Descent of Man*).
We find similar thoughts in modern literature: The Italian writer Alberto Moravia,
for instance, refers to the phallus as "La
Cosa" with which even lesbians are ob-
sessed. He also suggests, in another of the
Erotic Tales, that, in our phallocentric universe, a mystic—indeed reverential—attitude by women toward the male organ is a
prerequisite for defeating murderous impulses.

Sylvia Plath writes in her *Journal:* "My
greatest trouble is jealousy. I am jealous of
men, a dangerous and subtle envy which
can corrode any relationship. It is an envy
born of the desire to be active and doing,
not passive." So agonizing is this desire in
contemporary women that, compounded
by a striving to make of man merely a re-
dundant edge, it might lead one day to a
new scheme of things. Indeed, it is not in-
conceivable that in some distant future neo-

endocrinologists, together with genetic en-
gineers, should discover a special hormone
in the male organ, that this hormone then
be isolated, grown in laboratory conditions,
and ultimately developed into a "masculine
package"—to thrive and function indepen-
dently and individually, and to be picked
up at the freezer of a supermarket. It
would satisfy both the misogamy of some
of today's women and the perplexing desire
of others to procreate without matrimony.
Utopia? Haven't we achieved gene-cloning?
Haven't we detected signs of extrasensory
perception in green leaves? And haven't we
recently recognized secret signals between
trees, alerting each other of approaching
danger? We have also ascertained that the
female lizard can lay eggs without being
fertilized by a male and that stick-insects
can propagate for generations without any
male help at all.

As to the orexis of sex, if the eugenicists
have their way, the joys of intercourse and
Nature's mandate to procreate will be completely separated. Some women might
choose their "masculine package" for sex-

ual self-gratification, while their maternal needs—met at the supermarket as well—would be taken care of by sperm banks in multiple selections, to suit their individual tastes. Women might also find a way to subdue their sexual longing. Before Cecrops, who, according to Greek legend, was the founder of Athens, children were ignorant of their fathers. For that ancient people, the word and concept of "father" did not exist. Nor was women's main desire marital bliss; they only wished for fertility and procreation.

When the two daughters of Lot (nephew of Abraham) decided to copulate with their father, they had neither incest nor the need for a father on their minds. All they were after, according to the Bible, was to "preserve the seed of our father," who had no male offspring. The Ammorites and Moabites were the fruit of this intercourse. Nowadays, planned fatherless children are a commonplace; a large number of Lesbian couples resort to artificial insemination with the help of sperm donors.

Woman's yearning for sameness with man will never, never be fulfilled, unless advance science—already on the brink of altering life—shatters the inherent biological differences between the impregnator and the impregnated and contrives a new *Homo sapiens*. The new species would consist of beings endowed with both sexes, who—like the land snail in which the organs of both sexes exist in symbiosis—would be able to copulate with either. This would bring us back to the original androgynous stage antedating the *Homo sapiens*.

Men have had such visions since time immemorial. Ceramics depicting hermaphrodites inserting their penis into their own vulva have been discovered by archeologists and attributed to the Mochica and Galinaz cultures of Peru (450-200 B.C.). Gene-cloning and embryo-transfer—practices which retain the structure of the species—will not solve the conflict between the sexes; they will instead perpetuate and perhaps even sharpen the dichotomy. Nor

Front and back of a Japanese
memorial. The inscription
reads: "Showa 36 (year of the
emperor's rule), January 14,
1961."

- Pablo Ruiz Picasso (1881-1973).
Etching from the series *Sueño
y mentira de Franco* (Dream and
Lie of Franco), 1937.

will the recent striving for parthenogenetic reproduction—aimed at doing away with the services of the male—gratify the majority of women. So, until a dare-devil genetic leap occurs, the penis and its flaunty erection will remain the point of contention between man and woman.

So much for the sensual aspect of sex differentiation. But what about a change in the mind itself, to fit a possible new species? A time may come when Scientific Man, instead of trying to reach the stars, will turn his genius toward the beyond within, to discover humankind's own endowment for piety and honesty, for goodness and compassion, so that it may finally be free of the haunting fear of death and the enigmatic fear of an ever so elusive god. Such an alteration of the mind will naturally establish a perfect equilibrium between the sexes; the archaic taboos will fade away. If this feat is achieved through advanced biotechnology, the evolution of *Homo sapiens* may be shortened by hundreds of thousands of years.

5.

*H*omosexuality and masturbation, which have existed throughout the evolution of our species, may well be at once atavistic and narcissistic carry-overs from the androgynous state. Masturbation, which antedates coitus, is common to most primates. For humans, however, it is a form of partialism. Voyeurism (of which pornography is an offshoot) and trepidation at genital exposure arose with *Homo erectus,* i.e. when man and woman assumed the upright bipedal posture; visualization and fantasies came later. Pederasty, together with male aversion to, or anxiety before woman—which Carl Jung dubs "anima"—is rooted in a yearning for the prebifurcation androgynous state of existence.

The Spartans' and Thebans' preference for males was only part of their intense misogyny. For the ancient Greeks, the passion of love could be just as noble when inspired by a male. Many considered the physical beauty of a youth between the ages of twelve and eighteen to be purer and more desirable than that of the female body. When Plato, in *Phaedo*, talks about human love, he means homosexual love. His disciples agree that love between man and man is nobler and more spiritual than love between man and woman.

Lesbianism, one might hypothesize, is the illusion of possessing a male organ and of wielding the supremacy conferred by its function. The swelling of the vagina and clitoris during arousal is but a forlorn attempt to erect a penis that is not there. Sappho, the great sixth-century B.C. Lesbian poetess, was perhaps the first to express metaphorically woman's agony at lacking a male organ.

Prostitution has its roots in woman's deep inner vindictive outcry against man, who, in a state of delirium at the bifurcation juncture, ejected and let go a part of himself. Originally, prostitution was motivated by religious votiveness, and was practiced as acts of repentance or to solicit favors from the gods. Later it evolved, in the West as well as in the East, into hetaerism.

Henri de Toulouse-Lautrec (1864-1901), French artist. Titled "Reverie D'Opium".

Rape, in which only the male can indulge (the female is limited to seduction followed by yielding) is a manifestation of man's constant possessive drive. It is the vengeful seizure of man by his bold and self-willed sexual organ, which, at the dawn of his life, completely dominated reason. It occurs because rut is absent in man, and sex holds him in permanent readiness for tension—so that he may escape from his noetic state.

Nymphomania is woman's intense craving for cleavage and dissolution into man, the primogenitor. Greek mythology tells us that the nymph Echo fell in love with Narcissus and, because he did not reciprocate her concupiscence, she pined away until nothing but her voice was left of her.

Some primitive ancient societies viewed the penis as a feeding organ and woman as a devouring creature with cannibalistic urges that could be satisfied only through intercourse. Fellatio, hence, could be interpreted as a spasm traceable to the embryonic stage of the human species and the baby's instinct for sucking.

Incest is only a relapse into an earlier ancestral practice. Hesiod, the eighth-century B.C. Greek poet, muses about Heaven's incestuous love for his mother, Earth. And, according to legend, Cain and Abel, the first offspring of Adam and Eve, were born with twin sisters, with whom they copulated and thus multiplied on Earth. Ancient Egyptian gods, too, much like the mortals, were expected to marry their sisters, and the Pharaohs of Egypt did marry their sisters or daughters, making them queens. Ikhnaton (1370-1353 B.C.) married one of his own daughters, and Ramses II (1290-1223 B.C.) married two of his. Cleopatra was nominally married to her brother Ptolemy XIV (47-30 B.C.). The Teutons, in turn, believed that their god Odin begot Earth by his daughter Jörd, and in practice the Germans married their sisters, too, until the custom was abolished at the end of the seventh century.

With the dramatic advances in joining ova and sperm without coitus, the prevailing perception of incest is bound to change. Fathers and mothers will be able to help

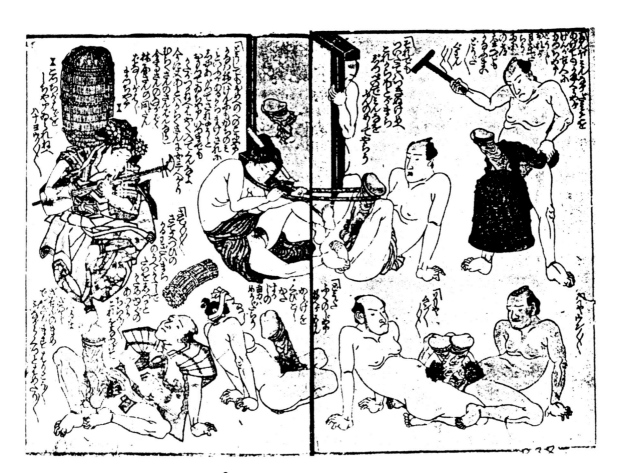

•
**Iwasa (nicknamed "Ukiyo"),
Matabei (1578-1650), Japanese
artist and puppeteer of the
Tosa School. The power and
rigidity of the penis is put to
test by strong women. From
Momonga. Throughout the
ages, the artists of Japan have
had to prove their mastery by
exhibiting imagination in their
erotic paintings, often magnify-
ing the size and power of the
penis.**

● James Gillray (1757-1815), outstanding English engraver. The
subtitle reads: "Presentation of
the Mahometan Credentials—
or—The Final Resource of
French Atheists."

sons and daughters procreate without the
angst of an illicit act. Russel Baker, in his
weekly satirical column "Sunday Observer,"
The New York Times, writes of science as
having "a picnic with the human embryo"
and suggests the following for a cookbook:
"Take an egg out of the ovary. Place it in a
dish. Add a pinch of sperm. When the mix-
ture starts to fizz, place it in a uterus and
maintain at womb temperature for about
nine months, or until noticeable agitation
indicates it is done. Remove and wrap in
soft cottons."

6.

No matter how many hygienic reasons are advanced to justify it, circumcision in effect is only another proof that man, since prehistoric times, has been greatly preoccupied with his generative organ. Some speculate that the mark of Cain, as described in the first murder story in the Bible, was actually the mark of circumcision. Most anthropoligists agree that circumcision is associated with the preparation for, and initiation into, the age of virility, the sexual act, and procreation. It may have had its origin in ancient Egypt, although some believe that the Canaanites—who appeared in western Asia as early as the third millenium B.C. and were ethnically and culturally related to the Hebrews—were the first to introduce the practice of circumcision into the region. In any event, the foreskin of the penis represented a blemish to a number of Semitic peoples in antiquity.

Yet circumcision—whether for the purpose of enhancing the human body or in order to confer a sign of full maturity upon man—was not exclusive to the civilizations of the Middle East. The Polynesians, for instance, considered it imperative to induce the transition from boyhood to manhood through circumcision, which, they held, was also necessary for the clean and virile look of the male organ. A well-circumcised penis was part of man's body beauty, an object of sexual attraction. It was believed that if the cut was properly made and the scab nicely removed, a more vigorous and thrilling sexual act and a richer orgasm would be likely. Maimonides (1135-1204) hypothesized that intercourse with an uncircumcised male could cause the female pain during separation.

In some regions of primitive Africa, circumcision was performed by the village blacksmith, without any formal ritual. The alleged reason was hygienic: A boy rolling around naked in the sand should not accumulate dirt in the foreskin of his penis. However, the cut-off foreskin was wrapped by the child's father in a banana peel and kept until the boy's wound was completely healed, during which period the parents were enjoined to abstain from intercourse.

- The Lingam-Yoni altar (representing the two organs producing life), regarded in Hinduism with the same reverence as the crucifix in Christianity. Here the altar is encircled by a snake, with a bull kneeling at the passage to the door of life. (4th century A.D.)

This gave circumcision an added ritual meaning. The Turu tribe of Tanzania forbade a male to have intercourse before his circumcision was performed, usually around the age of fifteen. And no woman was permitted to copulate with an uncircumcised male.

Among the Ngatatjara of Australia, circumcision was done, with a sharp flint, in veneration of their sacred kangaroo, and was accompanied by a ritual dance around a bonfire. In Madagascar, it was done in a subdued ceremony, to evoke ancestral roots and pray for sexual potency and fertility.

Some theorize that circumcision became a substitute for castration, which—as a ritual mutilation of the sexual organ in honor of the gods—had not been uncommon in heathen religions. Conversely, some early Christians resorted to castration to substitute for circumcision. This is attested to in the Gospel of Matthew, where men "made themselves eunuchs for the Kingdom of Heaven's sake." In the Bible, Elijah mocks the people who cut themselves with

knives and lancets till the blood gushes out upon them. Some of the Bantu people of South Africa to this day practice circumcision, to initiate boys into manhood. This rite—an occasion for great ceremony and festivity—withstood persistent pressure by Christian missionaries to abolish it as pagan. Up to the latter part of the eighteenth century, boys in Italy were castrated at a young age, to preserve their high-pitched voices for the papal choir. This practice was abolished by Pope Clement XIV about 1770. Celibacy, common to the priesthood in some Western as well as Eastern religions, may have its origins in the old castration practice as a religious mutilation of the sexual organ.

Of course, the concept of circumcision, or *Brith Milah* (covenant of the penis) is universally associated with the Jews. According to the Biblical account, it all began when Abraham circumcised himself at the age of 99, at the behest of God. For the Lord had declared: "Every male among you shall be circumcised. And ye shall circumcise the flesh of your foreskin; and it

Phallic lamp, copy of a Samian
earthen bowl; discovered in
England (last century B.C.).

shall be a token of covenant between you and Me. And he that is eight days old shall be circumcised among you, every male in your generations, he that is born in the house, or bought with money of any stranger which is not of thy seed." And so it became known as the Covenant of Abraham. With the passage of time and the awareness that circumcision had existed outside Judaism, the rabbis prescribed that in the event that a circumcised man converts to Judaism, a drop of blood be drawn from him as a symbolic act.

Thus, a heathen practice like the chopping-off of the skin at the tip of the male organ came to be regarded as a supreme obligation of the Jew and the stamp of his adherence to the Jewish faith. How important circumcision was to the Jews can be deduced from rabbinical texts stating that, were it not for the blood of the covenant, Heaven and Earth would not exist. At the time of the Temple in Jerusalem, only circumcised males could partake of the sacrificial lamb. Uncircumcised or testes-wounded men were not even allowed to enter the Temple: "He that is wounded in the stones or hath his privy member cut off shall not enter into the congregation of the Lord!"

Though in modern times circumcision is generally regarded as a prophylactic against certain diseases, in antiquity it was also considered a substitute for human sacrifice to the gods, an offering of part of the most cherished and valued member of the body. This is clearly implied in Exodus: "It came to pass by the way of the inn, that the Lord met him and sought to kill him. Then Zipporah took a sharp stone and cut off the foreskin of her son, and cast it at His feet . . . So He let him go."

The story in Genesis of Jacob wrestling with God on the site of Penuel also shows the idealization of man's reproductive organ as the seat of power. Jacob's "muscle"—so the Bible tells us—was touched in the wrestling; therefore, to this day Jews do not eat that part of any animal, "because He touched the hollow of Jacob's thigh in the sinew that shrank."

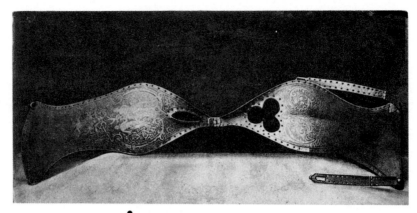

Chastity Belt, made of metal and used in Europe in the Middle Ages by warriors, to insure their spouses' fidelity during long absences. The belt was securely fastened on the woman and locked with a key which the husband took with him on his extended war campaigns. Musée de Cluny, Paris, France.

Yet, contrary to common belief, circumcision among the Jews was not always scrupulously observed. According to the Scriptures, during the exodus from Egypt and the wanderings in the Sinai wilderness, the Israelites omitted this rite because of the hazards of the journey. However, the Bible says, Joshua circumcised them with a flint knife, thus purifying them before they entered the Promised Land of Canaan.

Jewish sages elevated circumcision onto an anagogical level, arguing that God created man uncircumcised because He wanted man to be able to choose to perfect himself. At the time of the Prophets, the term "uncircumcised" was applied allegorically to the "rebellious heart and the obdurate ear."

Great art masters of the sixteenth and seventeenth centuries, such as Parmigianino (1503-1540) and Zurbaran (1598-1664), were preoccupied with the phenomenon of *Brith Milah* when they painted the circumcision of Jesus Christ. Rembrandt (1606-1669) was also fascinated by this ritual when he painted "The Circumcision."

Female circumcision, or clitoridectomy, is a heathen offshoot of penial circumcision. According to the World Health Organization, it is still practiced in twenty-six African, eastern Mediterranean, and Arab countries, where thirty million females are affected. This practice has come down from the oral teaching of Muhammad, known as the *Sunnah*, at the inception of Islam. Here, circumcision is performed either in a simple way—whereby only the tip of the clitoris is removed—or as a radical excision of the entire clitoris and labia. Either way, it is claimed that this genital mutilation reduces a girl's sexual desire and thus preserves her virginity for marriage.

Another prehistorical practice that crept into religion from myths about the phallus is the use of phylacteries, or *Tefilin*—considered one of the most sacred relics in Jewish religion. Literally meaning "safeguards," these objects consist of two small black leather boxes containing a Scriptural pas-

Vivan-Denon ? (1747-1826).
French engraver and lithog-
rapher. from the novel
Poliphilo. Titled, "Festival of
Priapus."

Henri de Toulouse-Lautrec (1864-1901), French artist. Titled "Les Deux Oiseaux" (The Two Birds).

Henri de Toulouse-Lautrec (1864-1901), French artist. Titled "Convalescence." An ill-fated penis is depicted humorously on his sick-bed while being offered a drink.

sage on parchment, and of loosely suspended leather strips. Phylacteries are an essential part of the *Bar-Mitzvah* ceremony, and are worn by observant Jewish males, from the age of thirteen on, during the morning prayer. According to some scholars, phylacteries were introduced into Jewish worship by the Pharisees in the third century B.C. Both the Greek and the Hebrew term contains "phyl" or "fil" (love), which—it is hypothesized—derives from the word "phallus."

7.

The shape and appearance of the penis played an important role in a number of civilizations. But, in contrast to the Jews, the Greeks of the Hellenistic period deemed a circumcised penis to be a body blemish, and some Hellenized Jews neglected or concealed their circumcision. Among them, a few who wished to participate in the nude in Spartan games, underwent painful operations to obliterate the mark of circumcision. Today, the retrogressive reconstruction of the penis—perfected by modern surgery—is performed only in rare cases when circumcision by electrocautery results in a third-degree burn.

Under Antiochus IV Epiphanes, when Hellenization was forced upon the Jews, a prohibition against circumcision was enacted, and mothers who had their sons circumcised suffered martyrdom. The resulting secrecy of the practice, and the difficulty of verification, eventually brought about a requirement by the rabbis that the piece of flesh so cut from the baby's penis be put in evidence as an open sacrament in the synagogue, for the entire congregation to see. This additional practice still exists among some orthodox Jews. To make sure that the operation was indeed performed and that blood was drawn during circumcision, the rabbis also introduced the rite of sucking, or *Metzitzah:* An honored guest applies his lips to the baby's penis, to draw off blood by sucking.

The fascination with the penis and its counterpart in the female has been omnipresent in human existence ever since man's cognitive faculties began to form. Thus it was only natural for early primitive man to interpret as male anything bulging or protruding, and as female any cavity, pit, or chasm—including those, or equivalents thereof, in vegetation. The Hebrew word for female in *nekevah*, which derives from *nekev*, or "slit." It follows that man himself began to erect or carve out—as symbols—pillars, columns, obelisks, or phalli, to replicate the male organ, while visualizing arches and domes, or oval natural objects such as flowers, fruits, seashells,

vestment, and to this day is worn close to the priest's genitals.

The phallus appeared in all places where fecundity was desired or sterility feared, and it was touched and kissed with religious fervor. Depictions of erect phalli in various shapes and sizes were affixed to tree trunks; they were also used as boundary markers and as protective and beneficial talismans for the harvest; and they were placed in temples, becoming central to religious ceremonies.

The Greek god Hermes was originally represented by a stone heap, which worshipers erected on mountain tops where the deity's spirit allegedly resided. Later, Hermes was carved out of a block of stone in the shape of a phallus surmounted by an anthropomorphic head. The statue was placed in the center of Athens, and came to be known as the *Herma*—a monument to the patron god of the *Agora* and of wayfarers and shepherds.

With the passage of time, the mystery of human eroticism and of the urge for procreation found expression in, and rose to, loftier, more abstractified representational visions than those of the early civilizations. In a sense, the steeples and naves of churches, and the minarets and domes of mosques, took on the symbolism of reaching to the skies. In turn, Frank Lloyd Wright questioned the need for reaching to the Heavens. Why not reach for man himself, he asked. To be sure, his churches have no steeples or domes.

And just as other art disciplines which did not escape the expression of human eroticism, architecture, or building design—admittedly or not—did not prove immune to the erotic instinct of man. Sexual visualization in structures can also be found in modern times. Indeed, Robert Twombly, in *Louis Sullivan, His Life and Work,* sees in some of the designs of Louis Sullivan (1856-1924) expressions of the architect's own sexuality and "maleness turning femaleness." Twombly even conjectures that Sullivan's designs suggest a repressed homosexuality.

8.

*F*or its strutting virility—and as a supreme symbol of Nature's magical reproductive power—the ithyphallus, or erect phallus, was universally worshipped as early as the Neolithic Age. Egyptian, Greek, and Roman mythologies—as most other ancient cults—drew their force primarily from gods of generation—with the phallus, as representing the penis, in the center. The sight of an oversized male genital organ provoked no obscene thoughts or ridicule. On the contrary, the phallus, prominently displayed, enjoyed distinction as a human-like deity which man venerated and whom he implored for help in the great arcanum of life. In the words of William James, "this integrity of the instinctive reactions, this freedom from all moral sophistry and strain, gives a pathetic dignity to an ancient pagan feeling." In Biblical times, according to all records, it was common to speak of intercourse and of human genitals as one speaks today of eating and walking and of hands and feet.

The Bible alludes to man's sexual organ as the seat of power and a mark of man-hood even as it tells us that King David uncovered himself gloriously before his maiden servants. (Exhibitionism?) When reproached by Michal, David replied that because the Lord had chosen him to be the ruler of Israel, "I play before the Lord and will yet be more vile than thus, and will be base in my own sight: and of the maiden servants, which thou has spoken of, of them shall I be had in honor." And because of Michal's denial of the king's act, "Michal, the daughter of Saul, had no child unto the day of her death."

It was a common practice to hold one's genitals when swearing or taking an oath, the make the pledge inviolable. In Latin, the word for testicles and for witness is one and the same: *testes*. Similarly, in ancient Egypt soldiers would raise their tunics in an act of adjuration whenever the kings exhorted them to battle, to show their penises as a sign of virility. In the days of the Patriarchs, it was customary to swear to the truth by placing one's hand on one's penis. In his old age, Abraham asked Eliezer, his oldest servant, to put his hand

• Vivan-Denon (1747-1826).
Much decorated French en-
graver and lithographer. Was
director of the Louvre
Museum in Paris. Titled, "Le
Roi des Rois."

under his thigh and to swear that "thou shalt not take a wife unto my son [Isaac] of the daughters of the Canaanites." Jacob likewise asked his son Joseph to touch his thigh and swear that he would not bury Jacob in Egypt. In some regions (e.g. Syria), both Christians and Moslems would swear by God's penis.

As late as the tenth century, Olaf II, who served in the English army before becoming king of Norway, introduced in Wales a law under which raped women suing their rapists had to swear to the truth by placing their right hand in a religious relic while holding with their left hand the penis of the accused. It is said that in 1798, during the Franco-Egyptian War, the then Egyptian ruler uncovered his organ before the French general Kléber while giving his oath of loyalty. And to this day, among the Eastern peoples, especially those of the Moslem faith, there are men who touch the lower part of their bodies, above the genitals, as a gesture of greeting or loyalty.

9. _____

Lacking scientific explanations, the ancient peoples divided Nature into two sexes. Thus evolved the myth of Father Heaven and Mother Earth, of a male injecting fertilizing rain into the vulva of a recumbant female, causing her to teem with all living things. And so came Zeus from Heaven to impregnate Alcmene—a celestial father and an earthly mother.

The ancient Egyptians considered Osiris to be the Sun God, and his sister Isis, the Moon God. Osiris symbolized the masculine begetting principle of Nature, and he was often featured with three erect phalli—to emphasize his power and vigor—while Isis was perceived as the passive female subordinated to, and existing only for the pleasure of, Osiris. The red-blossom lotus, which opens at sunrise and closes at sunset, was Egypt's most sacred plant, symbolic of the rising and setting sun.

In our day, the playwright David H. Hwang depicts nations in terms of gender. His Broadway play "M. Butterfly" contains the following statement: "The West thinks of itself as masculine. . . The East is feminine . . . , weak, delicate, poor . . . , but good at art, and full of inscrutable wisdom. . . , the feminine mystique."

According to Egyptian theogony, Isis copulated with her brother Osiris while still in the womb of their mother, and they begot Horus, who, some believe, later evolved into the Apollo of the Greeks. But it was Osiris, the male, who conquered all Egypt and became the Sun God—a culture divinity, creator of all matter, and the father of gods and men. Plutarch (A.D. 46-120), the Greek biographer, tells us that the Egyptians represented Osiris as holding with his right hand his big erect organ, as a sign of generative and prolific power and the source of the ejaculation that produced both men and animals. When Osiris's enemy Set cut him to pieces and threw his genitals into the Nile, Osiris's sister Isis assembled the fractions of her brother's male organ in order to copulate with him once again.

In a pageant celebrating his return from

• **Kitagawa Utamaro (1753-1806), Japanese, one of the most influential artists of the school of "Pictures and the Floating World" (the UKIYO-E School), famed for his depiction of beautiful women. Here two nude women are preparing for sexual activities with an artificial penis. Artificial gadgets (known as *dildos* 450-360 B.C. and mentioned in Aristophanes's comedy *Lysistrata*), originated with the Milesians and were universally used by lesbians.**

war, Dieceopolis, the fourth century B.C. tyrant, ordered his phallus-bearing slaves: "Come now line up . . . a few steps forward, basket bearers! Hold the phallus good and straight, Xanthias! . . . Both of you must stand up good and straight, both you and the phallus . . . and I'll follow singing the song of the phallus."

In Greek mythology, Dionysus—the god of wine and sensuality who was worshiped with orgiastic rites—copulated with Aphrodite, and she gave birth to a child with a *membrum virile* of enormous size.

10.

The human penis was not the only penis to be deified. Herodotus tells us that in ancient Egypt a living goat called Mendes was fed milk and honey, and kept in public places. Ecstatic women, hopeful of attaining fecundity, would give themselves to the goat in coitus. One historian of antiquity remarks that Mendes became so satiated with the many beautiful naked women surrounding him that he could be "inflamed" only by his she-goat.

Both in their mythology and in their daily worship, the ancient Greeks widely and explicitly figured the male organ as a mysterious power in the universe, and never attached an impure meaning to the symbol. The Greeks also painted, on the bottom of the inside of children's plates and drinking bowls, pictures of men and women enjoying various forms of sexual intercourse, so that the children could expect, upon finishing their meal, to find something amusing to look at. The male organ was also predominant in Greek conjecture as to the formation of the universe. The eighth-century B.C. poet Hesiod de-scribes how Cronus, the youngest of the Titans, separated Heaven from Earth with a sickle by cutting off the sexual organ of his father Uranus, who still had the strength to copulate with the sea and beget Aphrodite. (The word sex derives from *seco*—to amputate or cut off.)

At the Greek festival of Thesmophoria, which was celebrated only by women in honor of Demeter—the law-giver and goddess of agriculture, marriage, birth, family, and civil law—phalli and snakes carved in wood or made of dough were carried in a procession, to provoke sexual stimulation and invite public orgies. In the same vein, in front of the temple at the ancient Syrian city of Hierapolis, large images of the male organ were erected and placed at each side of the entrance—personifying the Creator who impregnates Heaven and Earth and perpetually generates and creates. So huge were these phalli-poles that worshipers in large numbers spent days on top of them, to communicate with the deity. The inscription on these towering poles read: "Bacchus has raised these phalli to Juno, his step-

Aubrey Vincent Beardsley
(1872-1898). Titled "Phallic
Fantasy," from *Dei Opali*.

mother." (In Roman mythology, Bacchus is the name of Dionysus, and Juno that of Hera, wife and sister of Jupiter, the Greek Zeus.) Within the temple itself, there were many statues of men with disproportionately large penises. The phallus endured as the symbol of Dionysus and/or Bacchus, to whom great festivals were organized, sacrifices offered, and processions and dramattic entertainment dedicated annually.

11.

Worship of the male genitals antedates all other idolatry. It can be traced to the very ancient Semitic peoples: the Assyrians, Phoenicians, Canaanites, and Midianites. Ba'al, the Sun God with generative and productive powers, was worshiped, among others, as Ba'al-Peor at a phallic altar, where naked maidens would offer themselves to worshipers in votive fornication. As the generator of all living things, Ba'al was represented first as a detached phallus, then as an androgynous figure. The historian Arnobius, who flourished in the fourth century, tells us that to evoke Ba'al, worshipers would whisper: "Hear us, Ba'al, whether thou be god or goddess!"

Perplexity over the gender of God and of the Son of God persists to these days, both among Creationists and among Evolutionists. The subject was indirectly revitalized only recently when the National Council of Churches—in its drive against sexism in the Bible—suggested for its new lectionary to the Scriptures the substitution of "Sovereign God" for "Lord God," "Child of God" for "Son of God," "friends" for "brothers" and "God the Father and the Mother" for "God the Father." The idea is not new; similar proposals have been made before. The American Unitarian clergyman Theodore Parker (1810-1860) made his Bible prayers read: "Our Father and our Mother God." The Jewish Reconstructionists have replaced "Blessed are you, God of our fathers" with "Blessed are you, God of our ancestors."

According to the Bible, Jews at one point, forsaking their Jehovah, lapsed into idolatry to serve the Ba'alim (plural of Ba'al) through offerings of phallus-shaped objects, fornication with Midianite girls, sexual orgies, and sometimes even human sacrifice. "Vex the Midianites and smite them," said the Lord to Moses, "for they have beguiled you in the matter of Peor." In Hebrew, *Ba'al* means "husband," "owner," "master," "lord," "coming-on." *Beilah*, of the same root, means the act of sexual penetration by the male. Ironically, in Yiddish—apart from "home-owner" and "landlord"—the term *baleboos,* of the same derivation, has come to suggest, facetiously, also "member of the gentry."

The Babylonians referred to Ba'al as Bel, or Belus; the Greeks, as Abello, or Apollo; the Gauls, as Belenus, or Belisama, wherefrom come *beau* and *belle*—say some etymologists. For many centuries, churches throughout Christendom were placarded with emblems of Ba'al and Ashtoreth (Astarte, the Phoenician goddess of fertility).

Serpent-worship, or ophiolatry, glorifying the generative powers of the serpent, was widespread in both Eastern and Western primitive cults. On the other hand, to the ancient Egyptians, the god Apap, represented by the serpent, signified the source of all evil. He inspired Set to murder Osiris. Traces of serpent worship—not alien to the Hindus, Chinese, and the aborigines of the Americas—can be found even among the early Hebrews. The serpent-charmer is but another version of the brazen serpent erected by Moses. The Hebrew word for the rod miraculously trans-

formed by Moses into a living serpent is *mateh* (baton), which also means "head," "center"—and is a homonym of "stretch" or "expansion." Elsewhere the Bible tells us that "Moses made a serpent of brass and set it upon a pole," to serve as a healing image. Ancient carvings discovered in Egypt depict Eve in the form of a serpent offering an apple to Adam.

In the heathen fable, the serpent whose head the Messiah was to crush, became the Hydra of Hercules, while in India it evolved into the great monster over whom Krishna triumphed. Roman mythology ascribes to Jupiter the slaying of a hundred-headed snake. Statues from prehistorical Peru depict prisoners of war tied up with ropes resembling snakes, whose heads seem to be stinging the captive's penis. Thus throughout history, the serpent—which so strikingly evokes the specter of the live male organ—has universally been both feared and worshiped more than any other creature on Earth.

Totemism, which conceives of man or

● J. Redgacsy, English
caricaturist, active in the second half of the eighteenth cen-
tur. Moses and the Ten Com-
mandments. The title reads:
"Moses Erecting the Brazen
Serpent in the Desert" (1787).
The phallus-shaped post at the
top left reads: "To Baal Peor."

part of his body as animal or plant, is prominent in ancient legends and primitive
folklore. And, because of his enigmatic incontinence, the penis has been represented
by various reptiles or other elongated animals. The turtle sumbolizes an androgynous being because its head protrudes and
retracts like a penis, while its oval shape
suggests the female. The erotic shape of
the swan's head and neck most likely gave
birth to the myth about the love between
Leda and the swan-transformed Zeus. This
legend first appeared as a sculpture in 360
B.C.

12.

In many civilizations, dwarfs and pigmies have been associated with the sex drive. In the early American-Indian societies, pederasts, transvestites and hermaphrodites, as well as dwarfs and other *rarae aves,* were believed to possess supernatural sex powers even as they were considered to be guardians of spiritual culture. The people of Pompeii, unlike most other ancient societies, used statues of dwarfs and phalli solely for the pleasure that their sight as common decoration afforded—free of inhibition and without religious pretense or deity worship. Until it was sealed off by the volcanic eruption of A.D. 79, Pompeii—under the patronage of the goddess Venus—thrived as a center of opulence and good taste, where sexual lust and debauchery had been refined to an art. The many unearthed Pompeiian statues, wall paintings, and graffiti bear evidence of a wealthy and pretentious merchant class and of a pleasure-loving aristocracy, whose preoccupation with sex and the exhibition of the male organ in numerous imaginative forms was part of everyday life.

The Babylonians, and later the Romans, attached to the phallus ringing bells *(tintinnabula),* presumably to ward off the evil eye and bring good fortune if hung up on the ceiling in homes or shops. The Norse peoples, even before the Greeks or the Romans, worshiped a trinity consisting of Odin, Thor, and Frikko—father, son, and mother respectively. Frikko became Frisko, or Frigga—goddess of voluptuousness—and was represented as holding in her hand a set of keys and a large phallus. The word Friday, with its many variations in the Germanic languages, has its root in this Norse goddess's name. The Gnostics believed that salvation for men could be attained through frequent sexual intercourse and the swapping of women. One of their sacraments consisted of virile semen offerings to the gods.

Although the Greeks and Romans did not invent cunnilingus, fellatio, sodomy, or the other variants of heterosexual or homosexual intercourse, they—who had made the phallus central to their sacred

• Multiphallic stones with wings and quails symbolizing man's productive faculty; discovered in Roman ruins at Nimes, France, as part of an amphitheatre's vomitories.

Dionysian rites—had knowledge of these practices, considered them a free expression of normal human needs, and included them in their hedonistic daily lives. They also established schools to train young slaves (Atanites) in the art of cunnilingus and the technique of fellatio, to make them more valuable to luxury-loving masters and their wives, as well as for use in male brothels in Athens.

The Greeks and Romans also associated birds and wings with the penis. Eros, the god of love, is sometimes represented with a pair of wings—which brings to mind Freud's probing into the erotic significance of dreams about flying. In the course of the archeological excavations of the early nineteenth century, many such examples carved in stone were discovered in the ancient amphitheatre of Nimes, France. The most outstanding are double and triple phalli decorated with beaking quails (birds whose odor is beleived to have the power of reviviscence). It is assumed that these carved stones decorated the vaulted chambers or arcades (fornicari) around the circus where gladiators gathered to relax with prostitutes after the games in the arena. Such gatherings were heralded at sundown by *tintinnabula*.

13.

*P*riapus, the Greek god of crops, cattle, and women—and of sensual pleasure—was a spinoff of *Ba'al-Peor*. As the son of Aphrodite and Dionysus—though his father refused to acknowledge him because of Priapus's ugliness—Priapus is generally represented with horns and goat's ears, holding a sickle in his hand and displaying a penis rigid enough to support a basket of fruit. He also appears as an elderly man pouring a libation in tribute to his brassy organ, to evoke a rich harvest. Priapus was the object of great veneration, and his likeness was included in every procession or religious rite. His sacred animal was the donkey, which symbolized sexual incontinence. Priapus became synonymous with the male generative organ or the phallus.

With the advent of Christianity, Priapus took on the persona of different saints, who were represented by large phalli carved out of wooden logs. These objects were revered and prayed to, especially by barren women, who would scrape the wood off the penis-like figures and mix the sawdust with water and wine. This they would

drink themselves or administer to their lovers, in the belief that it would bring sexual potency. In time, the wooden phalli in the churches would wear out from constant scraping and become shorter, and the priests would secretly extend them to their original size, to the mystification of worshipers. As at the Priapus festivals, worship often took the form of libation, with women pouring wine on the head of the phallus and then collecting the wine in vessels, to drink after it had soured. This drink was referred to by the French as "Saint Vinegar."

The worship of phalli-saints, which later spread all through Central Europe, lasted well into the eighteenth century, when it evolved into the practice of shaping phalli out of wax. Eventually, these phalli became simple wax candles. In some churches, wax phalli were suspended from the ceiling like mobiles: From on high, they would drip, melting from the heat, and would flutter in the air to the awe of spellbound worshipers. Wax phalli were sold both as relics and as olisbos—an instrument of pietistic masturbation. The practice of pietistic masturbation is implied even in the Book of Ezekiel, as the Prophet castigates his people: "With their idols have they committed adultery." Medieval Christians, much like the Romans before them, introduced a variant of phallus worship in nuptial ceremonies: The bride would sacrifice her virginity by inserting a phallic relic into her vagina, in the hope of averting sterility—since sterile women, even the most beautiful, were deemed inferior and even repulsive.

One cannot study the fundamentals of any religion without discovering phallic roots. For phallic images, in one form or another, have been the seed of all deities over the course of human history. No lesser an authority than Saint Hippolytus, the third-century Christian theologian and martyr, averred that all the sacred mysteries of religion originally sprang from a fascination with the male sexual organ.

Phallic images appeared in stone, on coins, on pottery, and on statues. Because of the fascination that it held for the masses, phallicism was accepted and often even encouraged by the medieval clergy. Ample evidence of the sway of phallicism over the centuries and across cultures has been unearthed in lands once dominated by Rome and later populated by Christians: Britain, Ireland, Belgium, France, Italy, and other Mediterranean countries. Early Christian churchmen readily tolerated fornication so long as it was performed in the name of an abstract deity rather than for carnal pleasure. Christian saints, such as St. René of Anjou and St. Giles of Brittany, became phallic deities, and in some churches consecrated to their memory one can still see stone phalli stained red with the wine once poured over them by praying women.

Evidently, mystical phallic fantasies were not alien even to the Israelites. This is alluded to by the Phophet Ezekiel when he admonishes women: "Thou has also taken thy fair jewels of my gold and my silver which I had given thee and madest to thyself image of male and didst commit whoredom with them." The Romans, who referred to them as "Facinum", used phallic amulets

•
**Von Daniel Greiner (1793-
1904), German sculptor. Wood-
cut titled "Das Leben attackiert
den Tod" (Life Assaults Death).**

**Von Daniel Greiner (1793-
1904), German sculptor. Wood-
cut titled "Leben und Tod"
(Life and Death).**
•

either as averters of evil or as harbingers of good luck and fortune. Greek tragic actors wore them as talismans on the stage.

Phallic jewelry pieces were sometimes made with wings, and worn as charms on bracelets or as pendants around the neck—the wings serving as a reminder to the wearer that coitus was only a devotion and a sacrifice in the service of procreation. To this day, in some small European villages, men wear gold, silver or lead phallus-like amulets for the magical erotic influence that they are alleged to wield. Children wear them for protection against the evil eye. In the European West, the phallus also remained an inseperable emblem of the clown until the fifth century, while in East Europe it endured until the fall of the Byzantine Empire in the fifteenth century.

Cobblers made phalli of leather, others crafted them from wax and clay—in all sizes, shapes, and forms; they were sold at church entrances. Women worshipers would kiss them and, in great devotion, offer them to the priest with their coin do-

nations, wishing for a large penis for their lovers. In small village churches, there were phallus-chairs for infertile women to sit in; at times, the priest himself would sit in the chair, to ensure fecundity. Phalli were also placed on house doors as talismans against evil influence and witchcraft. When in stone, they were used as land-boundary markers as well. For many centuries, France had a thriving industry of phallic objects, which were exported to neighboring countries.

Phallus-like masturbation pieces were sold openly in the market place. They are said to have been invented by the Milesians of Asia Minor. In his eponymous comedy, Aristophanes has Lysistrata lamenting that these items have disappeared from the market, causing anguish to poor widows: "Since we were let down by the Milesians, I haven't seen a single one of those rude leather instruments that have comforted us." In eighteenth- and nineteenth-century France, where these objects were referred to as "dildos," Lesbians of high society would fasten them to their legs for intercourse with their

- **Sampling of various brooches, often made of gold, silver, or lead; commonly used as jewelry by Medieval women. Retrieved from the river Seine in France (14th century A.D.).**

female partners. It is safe to assume that dildos were used by women both for self-gratification and to avoid pregnancy.

With the passage of time, these "artificial penises" underwent great changes. Today, in the United States and elsewhere, the market is flooded by sophisticated objects in a variety of shapes, sizes, colors, and materials. Some of these "pacifiers" operate on electricity or batteries approved by medical people. To lure customers, they are marketed under many whimsical trade names. Here are some of them:

Arouser	Anal Ecstasy
Fondle and Carress	Vibro Love
Ultimate Flexible Vibrator	The Trickler
	Electro Prickler
Butt Plug	My Fantasy
Anal Tickler	His Majesty the King
The Invador	
Foreskin Lover	Ultimate Climax
Eager Beaver	Swedish Erotica
Double Header	Jambo Jack
Baby Love	Anal Joy Stick
The Gemini	Ballsy Supercock
Upper Teaser	The Destroyer

Rough Rider	Vibratic Masterbation
Mystique	Power Thruster
Sir Ivanhoe	Manhandler
Sir Knobby	Corkscrew
Sweet Buttery Operated	Sensual Vaginal Aid
Ripple Vibro	King Fish
Silver Touch	Shaftman
The Phricler	Ball Buster
Slick Pleasure	Squirmy Rooter
The 10″ Dong	Slit Teaser
Bender	Solid Dinger
Ultimate Sensation	The 7″ Super Dinger
Spot Orgasm Vibrator	Vibrating Bullet
Dual Dancing Bullet	Stan-Hard Penis Aid
Vibration Galore	The Super Teaser.

As the conflict between the sexes intensifies and scientific discoveries in reproductive physiology expand, what we might term the "solitary womb" is bound to seek out a vinculum with an "artificial penis," and we can forsee the day when the dildo might become a common, self-contained, self-applicable insemination contrivance. Single women with a natural sex drive who are apprehensive about their biological clock, will be able to satisfy both their long-

Majestic monuments with re-
lief bases, representing the
power of the phallus, built on
the island of Delos, Greece,
(third century B.C.).

• Molded phallus vessel used for perfume, oil, or wine. The island of Rhodes (sixth century B.C.).

Bronze caricature of a Roman • with a phallus on the forehead and a phallus-shaped nose. (Pompeii, last century B.C.)

Bronze polyphallus with hanging bells called Tintinnabula.
These ornamants, often in animal forms, were found in the excavations of Pompeii. They were believed to wield magic powers and were widely used in temples as well as in brothels.

Bronze Tintinnabula. A gladiator fighting off the phallus-beast. From Herculaneum-Pompeii (first century A.D.). Like the Babylonians before them, the Romans attached bells to the phallus, presumably to ward off the evil eye and bring good fortune when hung up in homes or shops.

Bronze tripot with ithyphallic
young Pans on goat's feet, holding up a bowl. It was commonly used by the Romans as
a household work of art. Pompeii.

• Monolythic pillar representing
a stylized head. Southern Peru,
unknown origin and culture.

Comical ceramic vessel with
exaggerated phallus used as a
spout to drink spirits directly
from it. Peru, Mochica culture
(fifth century A.D.).

Votive stones, part of Roman
fortresses; discovered in York-
shire. Inscription reads:
"Priminus Mentla" (possibly
"Mentula," another name for
Priapus). Such stones were
often offered to Priapus. (Possibly of Pompeiian origin, last
century B.C.)

• Bowl with cover and three
phallic legs. Drinking vessel
with two phallic spouts. (Peru,
eighth century A.D.)

• Primitive vessel depicting fellatio in a guileless vein. Peru,
Mochica culture (sixth century
A.D.). The fellatio impetus, en-
demic only in man, has perse-
vered throughout the evolution
of the species.

Whimsical decorative an-
thropomorphic ceramic vessels
for spirits or water. Peru,
Mochica culture (eighth century A.D.).

Ithyphallic sculpture used as part of a fountain, with the phallus serving as a water spout. Pompeii (first century A.D.).

- Achondroplactic figure with large penis. Terracotta, Western Mexico (ca. 250 A.D.). Dwarfs and pigmies were universally associated with the penis. Statues of dwarfs straddling large phalli were household items.

Erect bronze phallus with human legs and feet, of Greek or Roman origin. Used as an apotropaic object, or against infertility.

Roman bowl with a phallus in
the center, to hold water (possibly for birds); Pompeii, first
century A.D.

Terracotta phallic lamp with a
faun-like figure, made to be
suspended in homes or public
places. (Pompeii, first century
A.D.)

A likenesss of Priapus weighing his organ near a basket of fruits. Mural discovered in Pompeii (last century B.C.)

• **Wall mural of Mercury, messenger of the Roman gods and protector of travelers and thieves. (Pompeii, first century A.D.)**

(continued from page 65)

mal's attempt to run away. The mandrake root was then kept as a good-luck charm, in the belief that a man's fortune would increase if the root were kept near money.

Even the Biblical Hebrews held that the mandrake had the power to bring fecundity to sterile women. The Bible describes how "Reuben went in the days of wheat harvest, and found mandrakes in the field and brought them unto his mother Leah. Then Rachel said to Leah, give me, I pray thee, of thy son's mandrake." In turn, Rachel promised that Jacob "shall lie with thee tonight for thy son's mandrakes." The deal was consummated when "Jacob came out of the field in the evening and Leah went out to meet him and said, thou must come unto me for surely I have hired thee with my son's mandrakes. And he lay with her that night."

Other peoples believed that mandrakes grew on sites where men had been hanged, for a hanged man's penis allegedly often remained in erection and sometimes even ejaculated sperm before the man's last gasp. The sperm, it was presumed, took root beneath the gallows, in the end producing the weird plant. The term *mandragora* seems to have emerged from such mythology, to be used as a synonym for the phallic amulets which Greek women and children wore around their necks from early antiquity on, all through the Christian era, and up until the eighteenth century.

The ginseng root is another plant which—because of its assumed resemblance to the male sexual organ—has for thousands of years been considered to be a miracle cure-all, an effective aphrodisiac, and a fertility stimulant. The rose, on the other hand, has since time immemorial been subconsciously associated with the female genitals. Even the custom of shaping bread in the form of the male sexual organ dates back to antiquity; it was common among the Romans who passed it on to the Christians. Old French cookbooks offer recipes for such breads and cakes, referring to them as *des cones sucrés* (sweet

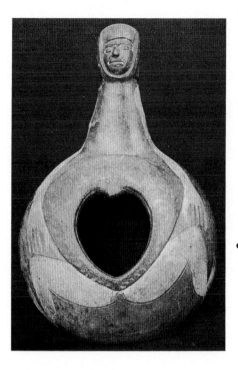

• Ceramic vessel with a woman's head on top, painted with her legs spread out and her heart in-between. Peru, Mochica culture (eighth century A.D.).

penises), or, if blessed by a priest, *du pain bénit* (blessed bread).

Like the Greeks and Romans before them, the early and medieval Christians incorporated phallic worship into their religious rites, to appease God and assure an abundant harvest. On Palm Sunday, the village priest would lead a long procession in the center of which a mammoth phallus would be carried in a splendid chariot. Women and children held palm branches, with loaves of phallus-bread suspended from them. The procession halted at the public square; naked women placed garlands of flowers on the enormous phallus; and the festivities culminated in wine drinking, singing, erotic dancing, and horse riding. There are many views on the origin of the legend about Lady Godiva, naked on a horse through the streets of Coventry, but the imagery has more than likely been drawn from the old phallic processions.

Greek comedy, says Aristotle in *Poetics*, developed "out of those who led the phallic procession." At the beginning, according to Will Durant in *The Story of Civilization*, these parades were simple celebrations of the reproductive powers, with a day's moratorium on morals. Many of the participants—in the Dionysian satyr style—wore a goat's tail and a large artificial phallus of red leather, and sang dithyrambs to Dionysus. This garb became traditional for the comic stage, and until the fifth century the phallus remained the indispensable emblem of the clown.

The penis also had great significance for practitioners of witchcraft and for secret clubs. During the initiation rituals, initiates had to kiss the erect penises of other members, and then all joined together to kiss a cat behind its tail. Secret phallic societies and fraternities with initiation rituals were prevalent in Britain and northern France. Common to all were rituals entailing homoerotic mummery and prickly rites—of which the ceremonial acts of today's British and American private clubs, and the hazing practices in some educational institutions, are direct offspring.

15.

The East, however different it may be in many respects from the West, reveals the same response to sex, fear, and mystery as that of all human societies. And already at an early stage, man in the East perceived his generative organ as the most overwhelming object in life.

To the Hindu, the lingam emblem represented what the phallus was to the ancient Western world: It commanded deep veneration. For Shiva, the most popular Hindu divinity, the arrow and the lingam were quintessentially identical, one and the same vehicle of energy endowed with the divine substance of eternal peace.

Yet, unlike the Greeks and Romans, who believed that the sensous omniously dominated the spirit, the ancient Hindus, like the Judeo-Christians, presumed that the spirit prevailed over all carnal temptation. The temptation of the flesh was—and to this day is—the root of all the segregation of the sexes. In one ancient Hindu sect, men who were called to high religious duty were expected to have their minds strong enough to tame such temptation. Priests, who often performed services in the nude, were sometimes terrified that the licentious images decorating the temple walls might cause an erection and provoke the worshipers to stone them. Even today, for fear of sexual arousal, orthodox Jews are not supposed to touch women, shake hands with them—even with the closest in the family— or walk between two females.

A temple in southern India, whose walls are adorned by many anthropomorphic representations, holds a huge stone lingam in its innermost cellar, or *garbha-grinha* (womb house). In the myths and symbols of the Puranas, this lingam is depicted as a fiery object or a shaft of light penetrating and fertilizing the *yoni* earth ("light is the progenitive power"). A cosmic sexual act is believed to have brought about bifurcation into two antagonistic sexes, which the Chinese term *T'ien* and *Ti, and the ancient Greeks, Zeus and Hera.*

Paradoxically, the Hindus, like the Moslems, visualized Heaven as a place where

• Girolamo, Parmigianino Francesco Maria (1503-1540), Italian painter. This circumcision
of Christ features the Virgin together with the prophet Sim-
eon as the *Mohel*. The painting
was done for Pope Clement VII.

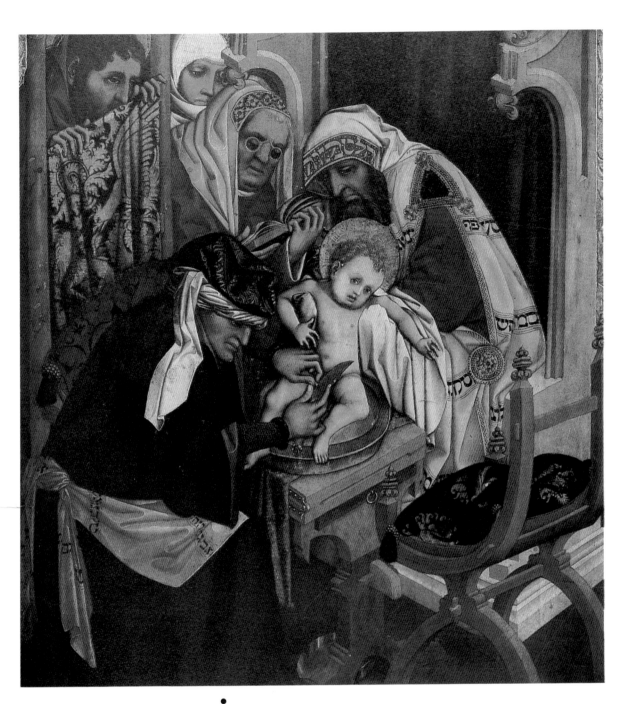

The Circumcision of Jesus
Christ, by the Master of the
Tucher Altarpiece, Nuremberg
(1450); depicts a rabbi seated
on a throne, holding the infant
Jesus, while a kneeling *Mohel*
is operating with a knife in
hand. A Pharisee reads from a
book, while the anxious Mary
and Joseph stand in the back-
ground.

• Eugéne le Poitevin (1806-1870), French artist. A devil and a young woman watering a garden, the woman is using his penis as a hose. The ground seems fertile with phallic plants.

Eugéne le Poitevin (1806-1870), • French artist. Blindfolded Cupid riding a huge phallus, with winged male and female organs in flight and women on the ground catching them in bunches.

man would be endowed—as his divine reward and for permanent sensual pleasure—with a supernatural penis producing a glut of sperm when fondled by beautiful women called *apsaras*. Medieval Hindu caverns were carved or decorated with such explicit images of great religious significance, for solace to suffering mortals. Between the sixteenth and the late nineteenth centuries, Hindu artists, inspired by these ancient images, devoted a great deal of their talent to depicting masterly erotic love scenes between men and women, in which the emphasis was not placed solely on the penis. In the strictly male-dominated world of the West, on the other hand, man's generative organ was usually represented as solo, unique, a self-propelled force, to whose imperium all else was subjected; the symbol of the vulva rarely occurs in Western civilization. In Hinduism, the *lingam* assumes the position of supreme deity only when paired with the *yoni*, the symbol of the female sexual organ, so that most representations of the *lingam* protrude from, or combine with, various shapes and designs of a stylized *yoni*. To the

lingam-yoni pair, regarded as the symbol of eternal principles, offerings of flowers, milk, and fragrant leaves were made.

Such duality without equality is evident in decorations of the inside and outside of pagodas, and of chariots intended for religious ceremonies. The decorations consist of paintings in bas-relief showing men with penises of prodigious sizes which twist like serpents around naked women as symbols of entrapment and subjugation by the loftiest and most irresistible element in the Universe. Even Hindu astronomy interprets the penis as dominant. An old Buddhist anatomical zodiac pictures thirty-two animal symbols for the parts of the human body; the horse, because of its incontinence, represents the penis. In some regions of India, the *lingam* was carved as a huge stylus of stone, and village girls, anxious for lovers, gathered around it at dawn to copulate. This stylus was perceived as a pillar of fire stretching from Earth to Heaven and beaming in the Universe as the symbol of the life principle that pervades the cosmos. For the ancient Hindus,

● Michael von Zichy (1827-1906), Hungarian artist and lithographer. Titled, "Studies of Women's Hands fondling the Penis." Through the ages, some artists sketched the penis as they would any other part of the human body.

genesis was a cosmic sexual act which generated the force that sustains, and will eternally sustain, the Universe, physically and spiritually.

Throughout the Eastern world, it was common for sterile women to touch the consecrated *lingam*. Portable *lingams* were also rubbed between the legs during prayer, to induce fertilization. Similar rituals were performed for cattle, too, to make them more fertile. According to an eighteenth-century French traveler to India, women, in the temples lifted their dresses and sat astride on phalli-like stones while uttering their prayers. Such acts of infatuation with the male organ were not limited to inanimate symbols. Intercourse with the

Maharaja, especially for newly wed women, was an act of reaching out to and touching, through the generative organ, the incarnation of the deity Vishnu. It was a privilege highly paid for.

This religious reverence for the male organ had many other manifestations. In some localities, the priest often left the pagoda stark naked, and walked the streets with a ringing bell in his hand; women rushed out of their homes and, in pious devotion, kissed his penis. A similar form of prayer was also practiced in some Near-Eastern regions, where every mature female considered it her duty, at least once a year, to kiss the organ of an old sheik.

16.

The androgynous view of the genesis of the human species was not alien to Far-Eastern cults. The Syrian poet Bardesanes, an early convert to Christianity, writes that during his travels around A.D. 200 he saw in India an enormous statue bearing the features of both sexes: The right side was male—with the image of the sun figured on it—while the left side resembled a female—with the likeness of the moon adorning her breast; the rest of the body showed paintings of mountains, rivers, plants, and animals. Bardesanes further related that the Brahmins believed that God had given this hermaphroditic statue to His son, so that it might serve him as a model in creating the world.

The Brihadaranyaka Upanishad, an eighth-century sacred scripture, describes how a self-originator deity—the very first divine being—experienced no bliss in being alone and ardently wished for a companion. Suddenly the deity realized that he was both man and woman in one body, and decided to cause himself to bifurcate by extruding from himself the female part.

After the transfiguration, he liked what he saw, copulated with the ejected female, and kindled life in the Universe. Thenceforth, carnal relations and procreation were looked upon as blissfully divine, for emulating the androgynous state of the primordial creator. Some scholars believe that homosexuality and sodomy have never been widespread in the Hindu world, precisely because of the deific aura of the act of copulation.

In representations of Siva, the Sun God and third in the triad of Hindu gods, the deity—closely associated with the worship of the *lingam* symbol—is entirely covered with serpents, the emblem of generative power and immortality. Legend has it that Siva's original penis was so long that it could reach his forehead. He later cut a part of it and divided it into twelve sections, which became the progenitors of the various races. It is also said that when Siva had lived among mortals, he was once surprised by distinguished visitors in the act of copulation with a stolen woman. Far from being disconcerted, the deity continued his inter-

• **Phallic caricature of the Comte de Honoré Gabriel Riqueti Mirabeau, one of the great statesmen and orators of the French Revolution. The caption under it reads: "These are the noble achievements of the count." Such drawings were anonymously distributed during the New Republic.**

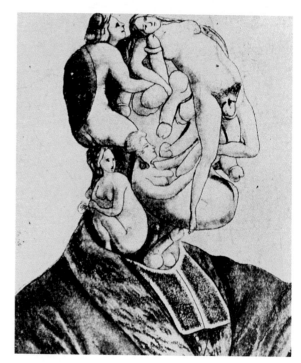

• **Phallic caricature of Cardinal Louis René Edouard de Rohn (1734-1803), French churchman and politician who was censured by parliament and disgraced by Louis XVI. Artist unknown.**

course, thereby offending the illustrious guests and causing them to cast a curse upon him—which froze the couple in the act and transformed both partners into a huge penis. Siva, the legend continues, accepted his new divine form, and decreed that, thenceforth, his priests spread the worship of the *lingam* as if it were Siva himself.

In the sanctuary of temples dedicated to the cult of Siva, there were columns of granite phalli illuminated by sun rays from a shaft in the ceiling. Around these symbols of Siva, priests in a deliriously religious trance initiated young women into the mysteries of love. Oddly enough, the cult of Siva evolved into a monotheistic religion, whose basic worship consists of vigil and fasting.

•

Félicien Rops (1833-1893), Belgian artist and engraver. From his "Satanic," engraving and etching. Title reads: "Le droit au travail et le droit au repos" (The Right to Work and the Right to Rest).

Félicien Rops (1833-1893), Belgian artist and engraver. Like the Romans, the French used the phallus to satirize royalty, the nobility and the clergy. This is a caricature of Louis XIV (1638-1715). The caption reads: "Tout est grand chez les roys" ("Everything with kings is big"). •

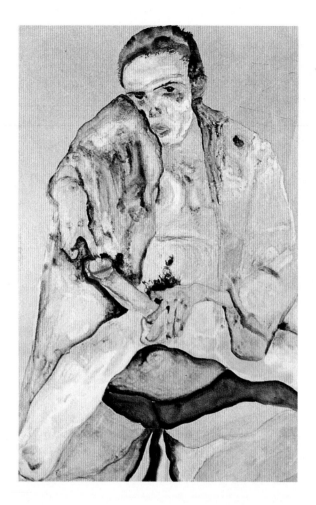

- Egon Shiele (1890-1918), Austrian artist, lived a tortured life and was prosecuted for his "obscene" paintings, but after his death gained prominence in the history of world art. Above is a morbid self-portrait, painted in 1917, toward the end of his short life.

George Grosz (1893-1959), German painter known for his caricatures and satirical treatment of Prussian militarism, considered one of the most outstanding artists of the first half of the twentieth century. Here is a self-portrait, one of his many erotic works.

•

George Grosz (1893-1959), German artist known for his bitter satire on and ridicule of the bourgeoisie. Here he depicts a woman helping a decrepid old man to masturbate; a phallic candle is at his bedside. The inscription reads, "La masturbation par la femme."

• Salvador Dali (1904-1989),
foremost Spanish Surrealist
artist. This water color showing dangling penises with an
eye in the center is entitled "St.
George Fighting the Octopus."
The inscription, top right,
reads: "Para mi Amigo, Carlos
Alemini"; signed, titled, and
dated 1963.

17.

The Dravidian Lingayats, who got their name from the worship of the *lingam* emblem, are a religious caste in the Bombay region; their divinity originated in the twelfth century with a holy man named Basava (meaning bull). It is said that Basava's unmarried sister Nagalambika conceived by the spirit of the god Siva. The mythical tale of this immaculate conception is that Basava, while engaged in prayer, saw an ant emerging from the ground with a small seed. Basava took the seed home; his sister swallowed it and became pregnant. As the emblem of their faith, Lingayats of both sexes always wore around the neck, tucked in a silk scarf, a silver box containing a stone phallus. Losing it was tantamount to spiritual death. Upon the birth of a Lingayat, the infant's parents sent for the Guru, the family's spiritual adviser, who hung an ash-smudged *lingam* and a garland of seeds around the baby's neck. The parents then washed the Guru's feet and poured the used water over the infant's *lingam*, to complete the baptism. When the child reached the age of eight or ten, the same ritual was repeated.

One also finds a similar concept of a heavenly male begetting an earthly female in the mythology of the Hindus about the goddess of love Sita, sometimes referred to as Parthivi (meaning Earth). Sita, to whom purified priests offered burning wooden phalli, was the beautiful wife of Vishnu, sometimes called Hari. It is said that Sita was not born of a woman: She sprang out of a furrow in front of her celestial father when he was plowing the earth. Statues of Sita have been rendered together with images of six kneeling satyrs holding their penises with two hands, as if offering their most precious possession to the wife of God.

Heaven as male, and Earth as female, are further evident in a Hindu symbol consisting of two intersecting ternaries (much like the Shield of David), which represented the merging of Nature with the Divine into an androgynous state. The triangle with its apex upward signified the active male, fire, and the sun; the triangle pointing downward stood for the passive female, for water, and for the yielding element in Nat-

•
Paul Margiotta (1951-),
American figurative and sur-
realistic artist. Titled "Adam
and Eve," this is one of several
in his series "The Beginning
of Man."

Salvador Dali (1904-1989), •
Spanish Surrealist artist. One
of his many erotic paintings.
Titled "Young Virgin Auto-
sodomized by Her Own Chas-
tity."

ure. To the Gnostics, the selfsame two-triangle emblem symbolized the intertwining of man and woman in a contorted intercourse.

The swastika, or Gammadion, in the form of phalli, was universally used as a symbol for the Sun God, but in India it also represented a polyandric sexual union and the path of peripheral forces. The Phoenicians employed a variant of the same symbol, which they called the Cross of the Four Great Gods, but it was the Hindus—

presumably the originators of the swastika—who rendered it as four distinct phalli with one female organ in the center. In Norse mythology, an object of analogous structure was used by the god Thor as a magical hammer, to consecrate newly married couples. The Edda section of old Norse literature tells us that Thor's phallic hammer was once stolen by the giant Thrym, who refused to return it unless the goddess of love Freya was offered to him. Thor disguised himself as Freya, slew the giant, and recovered his phallic swastika.

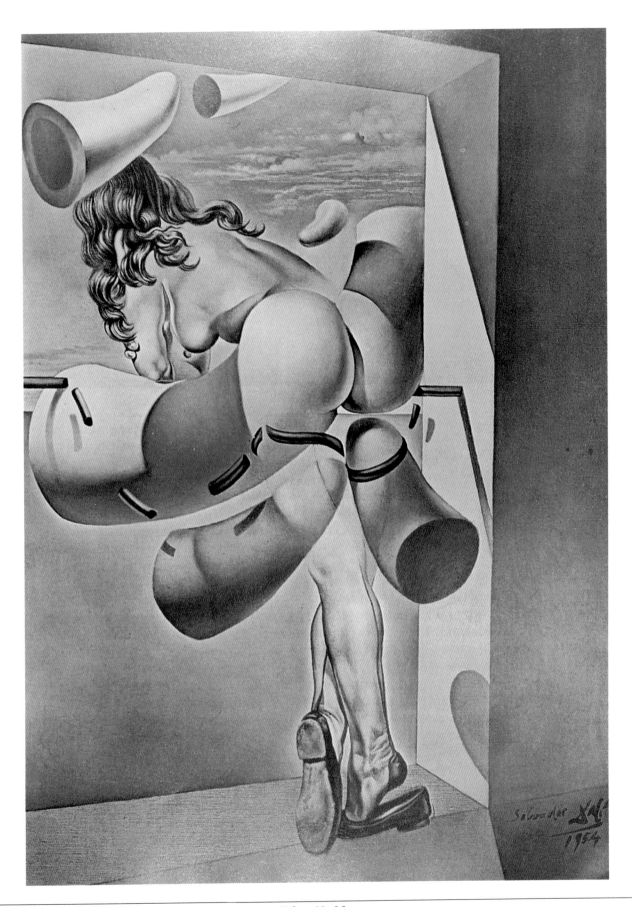

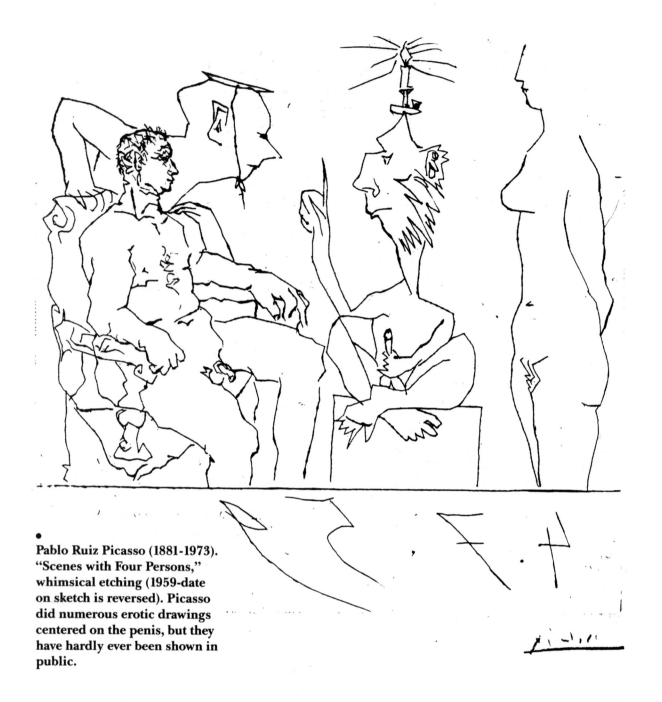

Pablo Ruiz Picasso (1881-1973).
"Scenes with Four Persons,"
whimsical etching (1959-date
on sketch is reversed). Picasso
did numerous erotic drawings
centered on the penis, but they
have hardly ever been shown in
public.

myth, it was formed by a drop of sea water that fell off the jeweled spear of the divinity Izamagi while he stirred the ocean.

Old Japanese phallicism attached significance to color. Bright red symbolized the positive and potent in the male, while black and the other dark hues were associated with the female. When good fortune came to a home, it was customary to cook rice with red beans in order to obtain *kewameshi*, or red rice, which then was shared with friends and neighbors. The penis also was a factor in the very process of cooking rice. There was a belief among the Japanese that by exposing an erect penis before the boiling pot, the steaming of rice would be improved and hastened.

20.

Phallic festivals were common—and take place even today—in some parts of Japan. One of the better-known is the Tashiro Jinja Festival at Nagoya, where a big wooden phallus would be paraded in the streets or in rice fields, to be ritually thrust into a straw-made vagina at the end of the procession—whereupon sake would be poured over the union. Another phallic festival consists in setting a gigantic wooden phallus on fire and immersing it in full flames into the sea. In some regions, during phallic games and contests, judges would measure erect penises and award a prize for the longest and most tumescent— a practice possibly rooted in the belief that the Japanese male, somewhat slow sexually, does not possess a particularly large or potent organ.

In Japan as in Western antiquity, wooden and stone phalli were once divine talismans to travelers. Such symbolic artifacts were put up at roadsides and crossways, to be worshiped as guiding gods. Phalli were prayed to, and, before starting out on a journey, travelers would offer them gifts.

Young women in turn secretly attached to them written prayers. Considered to be guiding marks to and from Heaven, the phallic posts were believed to have guided the deity Ninigi during his descent to Earth.

The concepts of original sin and of aberrant sexual behavior are alien to the Japanese. Their word *sei,* for sex, is a homonym of "holy." To them, naked bodies are less aesthetic or alluring than clothed bodies. In their sexual relations, they view the penis as a self-willed protagonist and the only part of the human body to be exposed—a view clearly attested by Japanese paintings of erotic fantasies. It is peculiar to the Japanese to train young girls in the art of coitus; they begin by developing in the female a gleeful attitude toward lovemaking and sexual play. Thus the word *warau,* meaning laugh, has been added as a prefix to every word in the Japanese vocabulary for sex and erotica. In the seventeenth, eighteenth, and nineteenth centuries, Japanese noblemen resorted to special geishas skilled in the more idiosyncratic or aberrant modes of eliciting male orgasm.

- John Altoon (1925-1969), American artist. Title referred to as C/I-13. The act of measuring the penis in this work evokes a number of similar Japanese drawings.

These girls also served as bystanders, merely to guide the nobleman's penis into another woman's vagina.

Perhaps the most incredible example of the male organ's powerful and mystifying hold upon primitive man is the *hiobbashira*, or man-pillar, consisting of a living man in a standing position, with his penis erect, to be entombed within the walls of a monument under construction, so that the building may be fortified and evil spirits warded off.

In Japan, where phallicism is obviously deep-rooted and widespread, the male organ has (at one time or another) been variously referred to as: *kishi* (turtle head); *yari* (spear); *ya* (arrow); *matsutake* (mushroom); *habi* (snake); *teppō* (gun); *shoki* (broom); *kagi* (key); *taihō* (cannon); *tengu no hana* (devil's nose); *suzu* (bell); *chinpo* (rare jewel); *shakuhachi* (musical instrument); *tōgarashi* (pepper); *ken* (sword).

In China, on the other hand, erotic nudity and group orgies have never been practiced, although in the past the elite classes had the privilege of keeping con-cubines and servants, and even used women as pillows to elevate one of the partners in coitus to the necessary height. Eighteenth- and nineteenth-century Chinese scrolls portray emperors on seesaws, swung back and forth by servants, as the ruler tries to penetrate a woman. Other illustrations show practices similar to those in Japan—concubines guiding the royal penis into another woman's vagina. Many Chinese scrolls also contain instructions or guidelines for would-be concubines on how to increase the sexual pleasure of the male.

First in China, then in Japan, a helpful manual for lovers named the *Pillow Book* and containing, among other detailed illustrations, forty-eight contorted positions of intercourse, was used to teach girls how to manipulate the male organ, and was sold at market places; often it was offered as a gift to newly-weds. Some of the instructions contained therein were ritually inspired by common custom, which in China prevailed until Christian missionaries succeeded in causing Emperor Chi'en-Lung (1711-1799) to admonish against it.

21.

*E*vidence of phallicism in the history of the North American Indians is scant. In Central and South America, however, considerable proof has been uncovered to attest to widespread phallicism intertwined with a pederasty of a possibly sacred nature. In some regions of Peru (where human presence dates back 12,000 years), each temple or sanctuary maintained a number of young transvestite males, trained from childhood to speak and behave in an effeminate fashion, for the ritual entertainment of chieftains on holy festive occasions. Those most skilled in the art of homosexuality were promoted to the priesthood and became guardians of the temple. Within the now extinct Mochica civilization of Peru, punishment for any transgression under existing mores was self-inflicted and consisted in a man's voluntary refraining from looking at his own penis and of abstaining from sexual pleasures.

No less pervasive is homosexual activity between an adult and a young male in today's societies. In Pagsanjan, the Philippines, many young children are encouraged, and sometimes even trained, by their parents to sell themselves for sexual acts with tourists seeking carnal pleasure. Residents, among them leaders, of that city welcome this practice as a necessary income to their poor community. Some parents are even proud of their children's accomplishments.

Possibly the greatest archeological finds relating to phallicism—some dating from the fifteenth century B.C.—concern the Checan culture in the arid regions of Peru. Most of the discoveries consist of vessels or other ceramic or stone artifacts with carvings depicting sexual scenes as religious rites—presumably intended to offer moral lessons: either to extol or to admonish against certain acts of man. These carvings, some of which inordinately exaggerate man's erect genitals, reveal sexual petting, fellatio, sodomy, and various positions of intercourse. For the Checans, such objects doubled as funerary offerings when they were placed in graves with the express intent of extending the sexual pleasure of the dead.

● Jules Pascin (1885-1930),
French-school painter, born as
Julius Pinkas in Bulgaria,
whose erotic works often deal
with depravity. Shows a
madame uncovering a bashful
transvestite before two surprised customers in her
brothel.

For, in the prehistoric Checan civilization, it was not uncommon for a living male to copulate with a dead female. Artifacts such as those described were prevalent in Peru, in one form or another, until the fifteenth century when first the Incas and then the Spanish Conquistadores emerged as victors. The Peruvian discoveries, made early in the twentieth century, have escaped world-wide attention, presumably because of the prudery of the Christian establishment.

22.

Nothing is as common to all humans as the sexual drive. Despite differences of race, geography, lore, culture, and mores, sexuality, with all its ramifications, is universal. At the same time—given the limitations of *Homo sapiens*—penis reverence remains the most enigmatic and subliminal of human experiences, and, consciously or subconsciously, men and women will forever puzzle over the nature of the male organ. Civilized societies react to an exposed penis as to something embarrassing, and refrain from referring to it directly. Yet, ironically, in the past the penis was viewed as the instrument of a divine act. Today, with such a variety of epithets for the penis, the universal intent is to express disparagement or ridicule. There is no language in the world that does not make one or another name for the male organ pudendum synonymous with either a brainless or an uncouth person. Could the reason for this be that the penis acts in his own unyielding and irrational way, heedless of the human mind?

Sexual intercourse itself is nowadays per-ceived as an act of degradation or depravity. Witness the many variations of the expressions "fuck it" and "fucked-up," and their equivalents in every language, as exemplified by the French word *cul*, meaning "buttock" or "ass" (in slang it also means "torpid man") and its derivative *je t'encule* (I fuck you), which, as in English, is an expression of contempt. In French slang, *couilles* means testicles; *couillon*, an obtuse person; *couillon mol*, a man without courage; *couillonner*, screwing up; *couillonade*, a stupid act. In Italian, the same insult is rendered by *chiavare*, putting the key in the hole. In Yiddish, the word *shmok*, meaning penis, is mostly used for "a gullible man." It is conceivanle that the demeaning connotation of coitus—when it is devoid of votiveness—is associated solely with the act of penetration. In the Bible, women refer to it as "coming into me."

One might conjecture that the male's hidden loneliness and guilt, as well as his sense of commiseration with the female during and after intercourse, are evidence of man's ambivalence about sex. Man feels

Aubrey Vincent Beardsley
(1872-1898). Titled "The
Examination of the Herald."

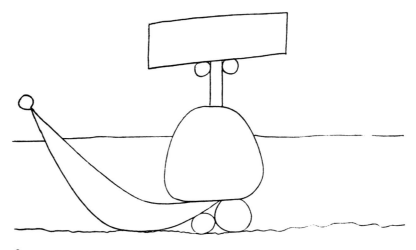

●
**Pablo Ruiz Picasso (1881-1973).
Drawing of the most rudimentary elements of the human
figure. Rectangular head,
baloon-shaped torso and a
commanding penis (1933).**

forlorn and beside himself when he is possessed by the penis, whether he be alone or with a mate. Similarly, woman's sense of obscenity during coitus might well be rooted in a cognizance of submission to a surreptitious act of debasement. In exchange, she often expects praise or gratitude; man in turn feels beholden. Was it Saul Bellow who said, "I never touched a fig leaf that did not turn into a price tag?"

According to legend, in a moment of contrition, Helen of Troy called herself a depraved bitch. The Greek nymph Daphne, to escape penetration by Apollo, wished to change into a laurel tree, and had her wish fulfilled. In a semidisguised lamentation about the woes of her female existence, Germaine Greer, with sharp sagacity, postulated: "Every man should be fucked into the ass, so he knows what it feels like to be penetrated."

In *Pornography,* Andrea Dworkin also castigates male abuse of the female: "Pornography reveals that male pleasure is inextricably tied to victimizing, hunting, exploit-

ing." Is there a difference between the perversion of pornography and other forms of erotica? In ancient societies, where natural human instincts and impulses were interfused with votiveness, the perception of pornography as such did not exist. Sex and violence were never combined. The Greeks and Romans were innocent of obscenity in their eroticism, whether one looks at their mythologies or at their practices. It is within puritan societies—because of the concepts of sin and transgression and an inevitable hedonist backlash—that pornography flourishes. It would be safe to say that the profanation of sex today is part of the general violence in the contemporary world. And the unbridled roar of pornorock music, it too, has its roots in present-day hypocrisy.

Inevitably, carnality and debauchery between the sexes will go on, but when all is said and done, and whatever we may postulate about the future of humankind, the world will not be ruined by debauchery; nor will it be saved by the absence of it. It will be ruined by man's violence, in any

André Masson (1893-1987),
French surrealist painter.
Lithographic illustration to
George Bataille's *L'Histoire de
l'Oeil* (1928).

form, and, if ever, will be saved by the absence of violence. "Nothing human disgusts me, unless it's cruel or violent," says Hannah in Tennessee Williams' *Night of the Iguana*.

Pudency and embarrassment in sexual matters are an outgrowth of the socialized human animal's instinctive need for seclusion during the act. Most people are furtive rather than ashamed. Yet neither furtiveness nor embarrassment can be indiscriminately attributed to all the peoples of the world. Among Hindu and Polynesian tribes, newly wed couples indulge in coitus

Pablo Ruiz Picasso (1881-1973).
Untitled, 1968.

in the presence of assembled guests, as part of the wedding ceremony.

The sinful aspect of, and hang-ups stemming from, the sexual act as such were unknown in Greco-Roman times. "So did Romans keep all their sadness and gladnesses unmingled and entire. Instinctively good, they did not reckon sin; nor had they any such desire to save the credit of the uni-

verse," writes William James. The stigma of transgression originated with, and was propagated by, the Judeo-Christian faith. Maimonides suggests that the tenet of circumcision is for the purpose of weakening the organ and counteracting excessive sexual lust—which in itself is sinful. The Bible associates knowledge with the awareness of sex. Adam and Eve were naked and "not ashamed" before they were struck by

●
**Laszlo Roth (1921-), Hunga-
rian-born American artist and
cartoonist. Titled "Hal-
lelujah," 1987.**

"knowledge." Subsequent to knowledge
came intercourse, and therewith the notion
of original sin. St. Augustine—in the spirit
of St. Paul—maintains that, as a conse-
quence of Adam's fall from grace, the original sin was transmitted by the sting of concupiscence in natural generation, and mankind was penalized with an inherited urge
to sin. Kant also represents original sin as
an inherent tendency in man toward evil.
According to Roman Catholic doctrine, the
Virgin Mary's first moment of conception
by the grace of the Almighty was marked
by the need to spare her all the strain of
sin implied in natural intercourse. Thus
the Savior of the human race was himself
saved from being born through an act of
sin. And thus has the concept of virginity
remained synonymous with purity. To be
sure, the dogma of Immaculate Conception
did not become an article of faith until its
promulgation in 1854 by Pope Pius IX. According to Ashley Montagu, the very idea
of the Blessed Virgin Mary is a medieval
invention, and does not occur in the New
Testament. Nor was Mary, Mother of Jesus,
or any other woman, present at the Last
Supper, *Seder,* to share the bread and wine

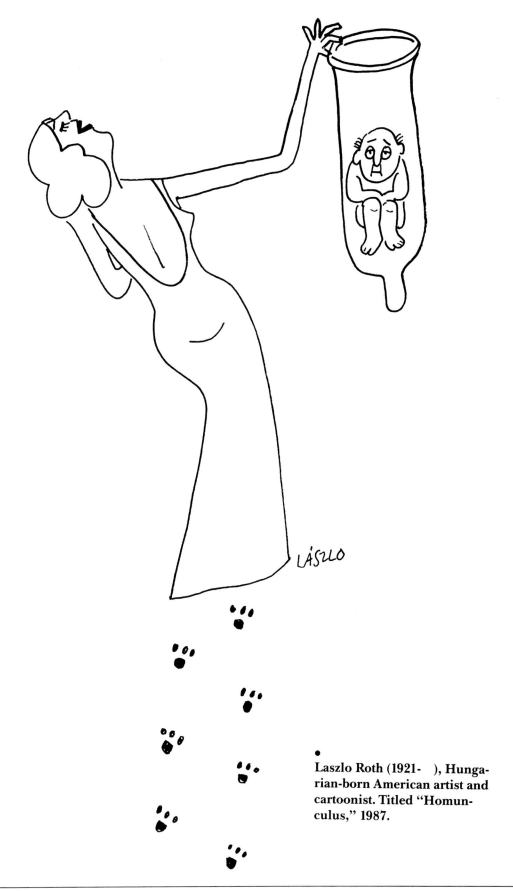

Laszlo Roth (1921-   ), Hungarian-born American artist and cartoonist. Titled "Homunculus," 1987.

that in the sixteenth century became the symbol of Jesus' body and blood in Christian doctrine.

Jesus himself, according to St. Matthew, considered the loving act as unchaste. He preached to his disciples that "whosoever looketh on a woman to lust her, hath committed adultery with her already in his heart." The apostle Paul, in turn, saw all sexual activity as lust.

The Christian Church, since its foundation and up to this day, has relegated women to a secondary place. Interestingly, a medieval anti-Jewish Christian curse, known as the "Curse of the Twelve Tribes," condemned all male descendents of the Biblical tribes—for the Crucifixion of Jesus—to perpetual menstruation, as if they were women.

The *Mishnah* (Tractate Avoth) directs: "Engage not in much gossip with womankind. They said this of one's own wife; how much more to the wife of one's fellow! Hence the sages have said, Whensoever, a man engages in much gossip with womankind he brings evil upon himself [and] neglects the study of the Torah, and in the end will inherit Gehenna."

Even the natural sensation of pleasure derived by body contact during copulation between a man and his wife is disallowed. According to the Talmud, a man must lean on his hands and not lie flat upon his spouse, so that the act may be consummated only for the purpose of procreation.

23.

Procreation and the natural desire for offspring are an instinctive manifestation by the male of his sustained virility which, in turn, has brought about polygamy and surrogacy.

Surrogate motherhood (without the modern technique) has existed since time immemorial in the form of polygamy and concubinage. The first specific record of surrogate motherhood dates from the second millennium B.C. and is to be found in Genesis (16): "Sarah said unto Abraham [when he was four score and six], Behold now the Lord hath restrained me from bearing; I pray thee, go in unto my maid [Hagar the Egyptian] may be that I may obtain children by her. And Abraham hearkened to the voice of Sarah." The Bible further tells us how this surrogacy brought about acrimony between the Patriarch and his spouse.

One could also view polyandry as a form of surrogacy in that one woman bears children to each of several men (mostly brothers). Polyandry, often associated with endogamy (marriage within the family), was found to have been practiced by the people of Tibet, by the oboriginal tribes of Tadas in Madras, by the Gilyaks of Siberia and others. The precise origin of monogamy has been lost in antiquity. It is safe to assume, however, that monogamy has existed alongside polygamy at all times. Concubinage, or cohabitation, is currently referred to as consensual union.

Strange as it may seem, the Catholic Church (and churches of other denominations) had no specific dictum against polygamy even as they viewed it as morally illicit. Until the seventeenth century, a person whose wife was barren could obtain a papal license to take a second wife. As late as 1950, Pope Pius XII wrote an Ecclesiastical Pronouncement to strengthen the Church's opposition to polygamy.

The Bible, without recommending it, authorized a polygamous society for the Jews. In Biblical times, polygamy and concubinage were prevalent, especially among kings and the upper classes of the tribes,

● **Hindu arch, with the Lingham seen through the Yoni, in the form of a Greek Omega.**

until it was prohibited by Ben Yehuda Gershon (965-1028), a notable rabbinic scholar known as *Meor Golah* (Beacon of the Diaspora). His prohibition was binding upon European Ashkenazi Jews, but polygamy remained legal among Oriental Jews. In Israel, in the absence of a religious interdiction, monogamy is enforced by secular law, although polygamous immigrant families are tolerated.

Polygamy has received the sanction of organized religion in Mohammedanism and Mormonism. With the first, the practice was a carryover from pre-Koran times, while the Mormon Church promulgated it in its official doctrine in 1852 at a time when no law against the practice of polygamy existed in the United States. The Edmunds Act of 1882 banned Mormon polygamy on the grounds that this practice lacked religious rectitude and was devoid of the "divine inspiration" that Mormons claimed. In 1887 the Edmunds Act was broadened to exclude polygamists from public office, barring them as jurors and denying them their voting rights.

Both polygamy and concubinage have been erroneously attributed to immorality or to a lecherous state of mind in the dominant male. Sexual activity outside monogamy is in general a physiological need of the male to satisfy his libidinous impetus, which sometimes he cannot gratify with an only wife or a single companion. And because of this uncontrollable impetus or "sex drive," man's rationality is at times dimmed, which leads to broken lives and shattered marriages. History is full of instances of destroyed careers of celebrated clergymen or politicians because of what is called "infidelity" or "sin" (today dubbed "womanizing"). The recent cases of Rev. Jim Bakker and Senator Gary Hart are good examples. Modern psychologists perceive it as "man's tragic flaw" or a "death wish," and the whole issue might well be consigned to the domain of mental research and genetic engineering rather than leave it in the hands of the law, religion, or the media. All of this attests once more to chemical affinity differences between the sexes.

24.

Some of the old beliefs and superstitions about the mystic power of the genitalia prevail to this day. The Christmas tree, the horseshoe, and the mistletoe—considered to wield magical powers either as averters of evil or as harbingers of great fortune—can be traced back to phallic symbolism. The horseshoe and mistletoe are vulviform, and were originally paired with a phallus hanging in a central place of congregation. They appeared on boughs of sacred trees and as ornaments in churches at Christmas time; under them sexual orgies were conducted. The horseshoe became a good-luck object when it was nailed on a house door or was carried in a bracelet or necklace. The mistletoe, like the Maypole, became a house decoration, under which kisses are exchanged. It is conceivable that the mistletoe once represented the hair around the penis. D.H. Lawrence, who, like Robert Burns, treats his organ with great fondness and compassion, seems to make a similar point when he has Lady Chatterley describe the "love hair" around her lover's penis as a lovely "little bush of bright red gold mistletoe."

The gesture of placing the thumb between the index and middle fingers (also referred to as "fig") can be traced—on the basis of excavated amulets depicting the thumb as a phallus between two legs—all the way back to antiquity. Other gestures can be traced to Roman times, when harlots, sitting at their windows, used to solicit passers-by by forming a ring with their thumb and index finger. Willing customers on the street would acknowledge the proposition by holding up a finger as the analogue of erection. The gesture of extending the middle finger and clinching the rest of the hand stands for contempt. It originated with the early Christians, who called the middle finger "The phallic finger." Former Canadian Prime Minister Pierre Trudeau and former New York State Governor Nelson Rockefeller, as well as New York City Mayor Ed Koch, used this type of hand and arm gesture in public appearances, to the stupefaction of the prudes.

To ancient Eastern peoples, the wedding ring together with any finger symbolized

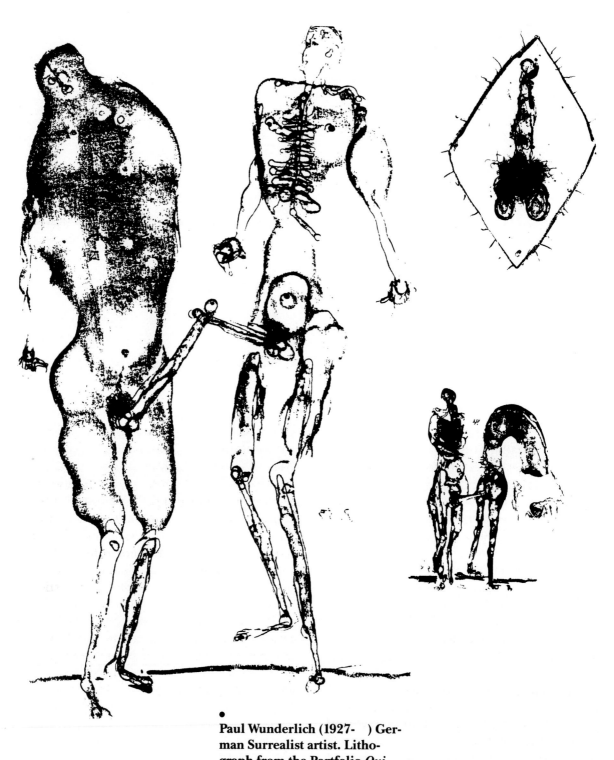

● Paul Wunderlich (1927-) German Surrealist artist. Lithograph from the Portfolio *Qui s'explique*, titled "The Sinful Deed Initiated."

the *yoni* and the *lingam,* and the act of putting a wedding ring on the bride's finger was—and still is—considered an act of conjugal union. During the wedding ceremony, the ring was often shifted from one finger to another, to enact symbolically sexual intercourse.

Modern phylogeny suggests that in the early stages of evolution, the hirsute man, like other animals in that era, was attracted to the female by the rutting odor of her secretion. Until—and even well into—the Pliocene Age, *Homo sapiens* exuded specific sex pheromones, or scented secretion affecting the behavior of the opposite sex. But, with the evolution of the species, that particular smell was lost in both sexes, and the female's odor for attracting the male was gradually replaced by artificial scents and fragrances. In some civilizations, the nose was considered a second phallus and the messenger of the testes. "Salute by smelling" refers to a mutual greeting achieved by rubbing noses, which is still in use today.

Just like the philosophers, poets, and writers of the past, great artists have been preoccupied with the mystery of sex since the beginning of art. The Egyptians were the first to carve and paint the act of intercourse, and in their art the penis was the main focus. The Greeks, Romans, Chinese, Hindus, and others did much the same somewhat later. Artists in Japan had to prove their mastery by drawing fantastic postures of sinuous acrobatic love-making. It is safe to say that over the centuries most renowned artists produced, at some time in their careers, erotic works centering on the male genital. In the eighteenth and nineteenth centuries, the great masters of the West completely stripped erotic art of its traditional metaphysical or religious significance. But because of the prevailing moral values of the Church, their works, like many other artifacts, were kept in hiding and were accessible only to a privileged few. Only in the second half of the twentieth century have some of these masterpieces become visible to the general public. Others, however, for puritanical reasons,

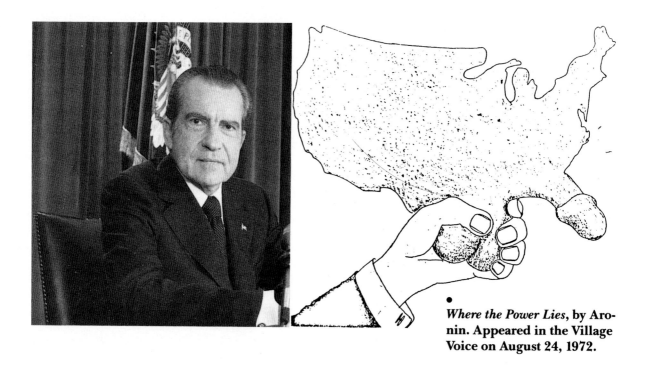

Where the Power Lies, by Aronin. Appeared in the Village Voice on August 24, 1972.

are still sealed off in museum and church basements (including those of the Vatican).

Representations of the phallus, referred to as *portraits d'après nature,* played a great role in France during the late seventeenth and early eighteenth centuries. They were extravagantly and lasciviously used for satire, ridicule, and to taunt leaders of society such as kings, political figures, clergymen, and men of letters—mainly as a reaction to the puritanism and hypocrisy of the society during and after the French Revolution. There is hardly a prominent leader of that period whose caricatured portrait has not been pictured with contorted, huge, and exposed phalli or in erotic design and positions of ridicule. The artists were often anonymous. Among the targets were: Voltaire, Louis XIV, le comte de Mirabeau, Danton, le duc d'Orleans, and Cardinal Rohan Soubise.

More than any other artists, Pablo Picasso (1881-1973) and Auguste Rodin (1840-1917) were masters in depicting the lusty pleasures of Eros. Throughout his oeuvre, Picasso seems to have been preoccupied

with the sensual in human experience—an affirmation of sexuality as a force in life.

One might say that in Picasso's wide-ranging eroticism, whether subtly suggested or unabashedly portrayed, all phallicism is idiosyncratically summed up and brought to culmination in modern terms. In his own words, "Art is never chaste." Some of his whimsical drawings, especially of the later years, depict ostentatious sexual confrontations between bearded minotaurs, satyrs, and picadors sporting huge erect penises. With other strokes of the brush, Picasso brazenly offered the phallus as a metaphor for the eternal key. And he has been quoted as saying, as if to emphasize the affinity of all great masters for Eros, that some of his own images represent a fornicating Raphael or a Rembrandt sitting askance on a throne. Most of these explicit works have been little publicized, presumably because of the still prevailing prudery of the establishment. Indeed, one would be hard pressed to find any major or minor artist over the ages who, consciously or unconsciously, did not express himself at one time or another in erotic or penial images.

BIBLIOGRAPHY

Alexander, William. *The History of Women From the Earliest Antiquity to the Present Time (1796).* New York AMS Press, 1976.

Aretino, Pietro. *The Works of Artino.* Milano: Mondadori, 1960-71.

Bataille, Georges. *L'Erotisme.* Paris: Edition de Minuit, 1957.

Bataille, Georges. *Les Larms d'Eros.* Paris: Biblioteque International d'Ecologie, 1961.

Baudelaire, Charles. *Les Fleurs du Mal.* New York: Harper, 1936.

Beardsley, Aubrey. *Lysistrata.* London: Beardsley Press, 1927.

Beauvoir, Simone de. *Le Deuxieme Sexe.* Paris: Gallimard, 1949 (2 v.).

Bettelheim, Bruno. *Symbolic Wounds.* New York: Colliers Books, 1962.

Beurdeley, Michel. *Chinese Erotic Art.* Rutland, Vt.: Charles E. Tuttle, 1969.

Bloch, Iwan. *Anthropological Studies in the Strange Sexual Practices of All Races in All Ages.* New York: AMS Press, 1933.

Bloch, Iwan. *Odoratus Sexualis.* New York: AMS Press, 1933.

Boardman, John, and LaRocca, Eugenio. *Eros in Greece.* New York: The Erotic Art Book Society, 1975.

Bory, Jean-Francois. *L'Oeuvre Graphique, Félicien Rops.* Paris: A. Hobschmid, 1977.

Borde, Raymond. *Dessins Erotiques de Jean-Marie Poumeyol.* Eric Losfeld, 1972.

Bowie, Theodore. *Studies in Erotic Art.* New York: Basic Books, 1970.

Brandt, Paul. *Sexual Life of Ancient Greece.* New York: Barnes & Noble, 1932.

Brendel, O.J. *Der Grosse Fries in der Villa die Misteri.* Berlin: Jahrbuch des Deutschen Archäologischen Institute, 1966.

Brolon, Peter. *The Body and Society.* New York: Columbia University, 1988.

Brown, Sengar. *Sex Worship and Symbolism.* Boston; R.G. Bedger, 1922.

Brusendorff, Ore. *Erotica for Millions.* New York: Rodney Books, 1960.

Bryk, Felix. *Circumcision in Man and Woman.* New York: AMS Press, 1934.

Buchen, Irving. *The Perverse Imagination, Sexuality and Literary Culture.* New York: New York University Press, 1970.

Buckly, Edmond. *Phallicism in Japan.* Chicago; University of Chicago, 1895.

Bullough, Vern L. *The Subordinate Sex.* Urbana: University of Illinois, 1973.

Clark, Kenneth. *The Best of Audrey Beardsley.* New York: Doubleday, 1978.

Cramer, Patrick. *The Illustrated Books,* New York, Banana, 1983.

Dahlberg, Edward. *The Sorrows of Priapus.* New York: Harcourt Brace, 1972.

Darwin, Charles. *The Descent of Man.* New York: Beacon Press, 1959.

Davidson, Nicholas. *The Failure of Feminism.* New York: Prometheus Books, 1988.

Davis, Nigel. *The Rampant God.* New York: William Morrow, 1984.

D'Emilis, John and Freedman, Estelle B. *Intimate Matters—A History of Sexuality in America.* New York: Harper & Row, 1988.

Dortu, M.G. *Toulouse-Lautrec et Son Oeuvres (Tome VI).* New York: Collectors Edition, 1971.

Dover, Kenneth. *Greek Homosexuality.* Cambridge: Harvard University Press, 1978.

Dulaure, Jaques-Antoin. *The Gods of Generation (1805).* New York: AMS Press, 1975.

Dworkin, Andrea. *Ice and Fire.* New York: Weidenfeld & Nicolson, 1987.

Dworkin, Andrea. *Pornography.* New York: Perigee Books, 1981.

Ellis, Albert and Abarbanel. *Encyclopedia of Sexual Behavior.* New York: Hawthorn, 1951.

Ellis, Albert. *Sex Without Guilt.* New York: L. Stuart, 1958.

Fiedler, Franz. *Antike Erotische Bildwerke.* Leipzig: Hinrich, 1839.

Ford, Clellon. *Patterns of Sexual Behavior.* New York: Harper, 1951.

Foucault, Michel. *The History of Sexuality.* New York: Pantheon Books, 1985.

Franzblau, Abraham N. *The Erotic Art of China.* New York: Crown, 1977.

Fryer, Peter. *Secrets of the British Museum.* New York: Citadel Press, 1968.

Fuchs, Eduard. *Geschichte der Erotischen Kust.* München: A. Langen, 1912-28.

Fuchs, Eduard. *Die Juden in der Karikatur.* München: A. Langen, 1921.

Fuchs, Edouard. *L'élement érotique dans la caricature,* Wien-Berlin, Benjamin Hartz-Verlag, 1906.

Gallichan, Walter Mattieu. *Women Under Polygamy.* New York: AMS Press, 1935.

Geddes, Patrick. *The Evolution of Sex.* New York: AMS Press, 1901.

Gerhard, Paul. *Pornography in Fine Art from Ancient Times up to the Present.* Los Angeles: Elysium, 1969.

Gichner, Lawrence E. *Erotic Aspects of Hindu Sculpture.* New York: Lawrence E. Gichner, 1949.

Gip, Bernard. *Katharina.* Geneva: Nagel, 1971.

Gonzalez-Crussi, F. *On the Nature of Things Erotic.* New York: Harcourt Brace Jovanovich, 1988.

Goodland, R. *A Bibliography of Sex and Customs.* London: George Routledge, 1931.

Goodsell, Willystine. *A History of Marriage and the Family.* New York: AMS Press, 1934.

Grant, Michael. *Eros in Pompeii.* New York: William Morrow, 1975.

Greer, Germaine. *The Female Eunuch.* New York: McGraw-Hill Books, 1971.

Gregor, Thomas. *Anxious Pleasure—The Sexual Life of Amazonian People.* Chicago: The University of Chicago, 1985.

Gulik, Robert Hans Van. *Sexual Life in Ancient China.* Leiden: E.J. Brill, 1961.

Hannay, James Ballantyne. *Sex Symbolism in Religion.* London: Religious Evolution Society, 1922.

Hearn, Jeff-Parkin, Wendy. *Sex at Work.* New York: St. Martin's Press, 1987.

Hemstead, Edward Charles. *Sexual Impulse.* London: Bariswood, 1935.

Hirschfeld, Magnus. *Sex and Human Relationship.* New York: AMS Press, 1935.

Hopfner, Theodor. *Das Sexualleben der Griechen und Röme.* New York: AMS Press, 1938.

Houseman, John. *Unfinished Business.* New York: Applause Theater Books, 1988.

Hoving, Thomas P.E., and others. *Art of Oceania.* New York: The Metropolitan Museum of Art, 1969.

Howard, Clifford. *Sex and Religion.* New York: AMS Press, 1925.

Hyde, H. Montgomery. *A History of Pornography.* New York: Farrar, Straus & Giroux, 1965.

Illich, Ivan. *Gender.* New York: Pantheon Books, 1982.

Inamn, Thomas. *Ancient Pagan and Modern Christian Symbolism.* New York: Peter Eckler, 1922.

James, Henry. *The Portable Henry James.* New York: The Viking Press, 1967.

Johnson, Paul. *Intellectuals*. New York: Harper & Row, 1989.

Kato, Genchi. *A Study of Japanese Phallicism*. Tokyo: Asiatic Society of Japan, 1923.

Knight, Richard Payne and Wright, Thomas. *Sexual Symbolism A History of Phallic Worship*, (1786 and 1866). New York: Bell Publishing, 1957.

Lance, Pierre de. *Tableau de L'Inconstance de Mauvais Anges et Démons*. Paris: 1609.

Larco-Hoyle, Rafael. *Amore Ed Art, Peru*. Geneva: Nagel, 1976.

Larco-Hoyle, Rafael. *Checan*. Geneva: Nagel, 1965.

Larco-Hoyle, Rafael. *On Sexual Pottery*. Geneva: Nagel, 1965.

Legman, Gershon. *The Horn Book*. Chicago: University Books, 1964.

Legman, Gershon. *Orangenitalism Oral Technic*. New York: Julian Press, 1969.

Levey, Louis-Germain. *La Famille Dans L'Antiquité Israélite*. Paris: Felit Alcan, 1905.

Levy, Ludwig. *Sexualsymbolik der Bibel und des Talmud*. Leipzig: Zeitechrift, 1918.

Lewis, Kennet. *The Psychoanalytic of the Male Homosexuality*. New York: Simon & Schuster, 1988.

LoDuca, J.M. *Histoire de L'Erotisme*. Paris: Le Jeune Parque, 1929.

Lucie-Smith, Edward. *Eroticism in Western Art*. New York: Thames and Hudson, 1972.

Lucka, Emil. *Eros: The Development of Sex Relation Through the Ages*. New York: AMS Press, 1915.

Mackinnon, Catharine. *Intercourse*. New York: The Free Press, 1987.

Malinowski, Bronislaw. *Sex, Culture and Myth*. New York: Harcourt, 1962.

Malinowski, Bronislaw. *Sex Life of Savages*. New York: Harcourt, 1929.

Malinowski, Bronislaw. *Sex and Repression in Savage Society*. Chicago: University of Chicago, 1982.

Marcadé, Jean. *Eros Kalos*. Geneva: Nagel, 1962.

Marcadé, Jean. *Roma Amor, Essay on Erotic Elements in Etruscan and Roman*. Geneva: Nagel, 1961.

Masters, R.E.L. *The Anti-Sex*. New York: Julian Press, 1964.

Masters, William H. and Johnson, Virginia E. *The Pleasure Bond*. Boston-Toronto: Little Brown and Co., 1975.

Mclennan, John Ferguson. *Primative Marriage*. New York: AMS Press, 1865.

Menzel, H. *Die Römischen Bronzen aus Deutschland*. Mainz, 1966.

Mirabeau, Honoré Gabriel Riquetti. *Erotika Biblion*. New York: AMS Press, 1890.

Mocsanyi, Paul. *Erotic Art*. New York: The New School Art Center, 1973.

Moll, Albert. *Libido Sexualis*. New York: AMS Press, 1933.

Moll, Albert. *Perversion of the Sex Instinct*. New York: AMS Press, 1931.

Montagu, Ashley. *Man and Aggression*. New York: Oxford University, 1968.

Montagu, Ashley. *The Natural Superiority of Women*. New York: Macmillan, 1968.

Montagu, Ashley. *Immortality, Religion, and Morals*. New York: Hawthorn Books, 1971.

Müller-Lyer, Franz Carl. *The Evolution of Sexual Marriage*. New York: AMS Press, 1931.

Northcotte, Hugh. *Christianity and Sex Problems*. New York: AMS Press, 1916.

Omlin, Joseph A. *Der Papyrus 55001 und seine satirisch-erotischen Zeichnungen und Inschriften*. Torino: Edizioni d'arte frateli Pozo, 1973.

Page, Denyo L. *Sappho and Alcaeus. An Introduction to the Study of Ancient Lesbian Poetry*. Oxford: Clarendon Press, 1955.

Pagels, Elaine H. *The Gnostic Gospels*. New York: Random House, 1979.

Pagels, Elaine H. *Adam, Eve and the Serpent*. New York: Random House, 1988.

Parent-Duchatelet, Alexander Jean. *Prostitution in Paris*. New York: AMS Press, 1845.

Peckham, Morse. *Art and Pornography*. New York: Basic Books, 1969.

Pelet, August. *Les Mosaic de Nimes*. Nimes: Clavel-Balivett, 1876.

Poliphilo [Francesca Colonna]. *The Strife of Love in a Dream*. London: D. Nutt, 1890.

Rawson, Philip. *Erotic Art of the East*. Buffalo: Prometheus, 1968.

Rawson, Philip. *Oriental Erotic Art*. New York: A & W Publishers, 1981.

Rawson, Philip. *Primitive Erotic Art*. New York: G.P. Putnam, 1973.

Read, Brian. *Aubrey Beardsley*. London: Bonanza Books, 1967.

Redford, Myron H. *The Condom: Increasing Utilization in the U.S.* Seattle, Wash.: San Francisco Press, 1974.

Remondino, Peter Charles. *The History of Circumcision from the Earliest Times to the Present*. New York: AMS Press, 1881.

Reutersrärd, Oscar. *Ritual Love-Making and Punishment in Egypt Myths*. : Edition Sellem, 1975.

Richie, Donald. *The Erotic Gods—Phallicism in Japan*. Tokyo: Zufushinsha, 1967.

Riediger, Carsten. *Paul Wunderlich*. Offenbach: V. Huber, 1983.

Riediger, Carsten. *Paul Wunderlich der Druckgraphic 1948-1982*. : Edition Volker Huber, .

Riencourt, Amaury de. *Sex and Power in History*. New York: David McKay, 1974.

Rostand, J. *The Substance of Man*. New York: Doubleday, 1962.

Runberg, Anne. *Witches, Demons and Fertility*. Helsinki:, 1947.

Sanger, William Wallace. *The History of Prostitution*. New York: AMS Press, 1939.

Schwartz, K. *The Male Member*. New York: St. Martin, 1985.

Scott, George Ryley. *A History of Prostitution from Antiquity to the Present Day*. New York: Medical Press, 1954.

Smith, Bradley. *Erotic Art of the Master*. New York: The Erotic Art Book, .

Soulié Bernard. *Japanese Eroticism*. : Crescent Books, .

Stern, Bernard Joseph, *The Scented Garden*. New York: AMS Press, 1934.

Stone, Lee Alexander. *The Power of a Symbol*. Chicago: P. Covici, 1925.

Stone, Lee Alexander. *The Story of Phallicism*. Chicago: P. Covici, 1927.

Suggs, Robert C. *Human Sexuality Behavior*. New York: Basic Books, 1971.

Sunieu, Robert. *Sarv-é Naz. An Essay on Love*. Geneva: Nagel, 1967.

Symond, John Addington. *Studies in Sexual Inversion*. New York: AMS Press, 1928.

Talmey, Bernard Simon. *Women: A Treatise on the Normal and Pathological Emotions of Feminine Love*. New York: AMS Press, 1912.

Tucci, Giuseppe. *Rati-Lila/Nepal*. Geneva: Nagel, 1969.

Vaerting, Mathilde. *The Dominant Sex*. New York: AMS Press, 1923.

Vanggaard, Thorkil. *Phallos and its History in the Male World*. New York: International Press, 1972.

Vatsyayāna. *Kama-Sutra—The Hindu Art of Love*. Calcutta: Medical Book Co., 1954.

Velikovsky, Emanuel. *Ramses II and His Time*. New York: Tickon & Field, 1978.

Villeneuve, Ronald. *Le Diable dans L'Art*. Paris: Edition De Noél, 1957.

Villeneuve, Ronald. *Le Poittervin 1806-1870. Diableries Erotiques*. Paris: Edition Du Manoire, 1922.

Waldberg, Patrick. *Eros in La Belle Epoque*. New Yor: Grove Press, 1969.

Wall, O.A. *Sex and Sex Worship*. St. Louis: C.V. Mosey, 1933.

Wallace, Irving. *The Nympho and Other Maniacs*. New York: Simon and Schuster, 1971.

Willoughby, H.R. *Pagan Regeneration*. Chicago: University of Chicago Press, 1929.

Zervos, Christian. *Picasso, Oeuvre Catalogue*. Paris: Editions Cahiers d'Art, 1955-1957.

Zwang, Gerard. *Le Sex de la Femme*. Paris: La Jeune Paris, 1967.

My gratitude also goes to The New York Public Library.

ACKNOWLEDGEMENTS

Edouard Fuch (see bibliography). Pages 14, 28, 29, 36, 61.

Ambrose Ruschenberger, Boston. Page 64.

Britania Romana. Page 15, 16.

Grenier/Maurice Exsteen Collection, Paris. Pages 26, 34, 42.

Christian Zervos, *Picasso, Oeuvre Catalogue*, Paris 1957. Page 21.

Associated Artists/New School, New York. Page 98.

S.P.A.D.E.M., Paris/V.A.G.A., New York. Pages 100, 109.

Patrick Cramer. *The Illustrated Book.* Page 32.

Private Collection. Pages 52, 89, 102, 104.

Victoria and Albert Museum, London. Page 106.

R.A. Harari, London. Page 55.

Gichner Foundation for Culture Studies, Washington, D.C./Ikeda-Shoten. Pages 35, 50, 86.

The Metropolitan Museum of Art. Page 19.

British Mercury (1787). Page 56.

Thomas Wright (see bibliography). Page 62.

Rheinioche Londes-Museum, Trier, Germany. Pages 22, 68 (top).

Donal Richie (see bibliography). Page 20, 31.

Lazzlo Roth, New York. Pages 110, 111.

Tibor de Nagi Gallery/New School, New York. Page 102.

Aronin/Village Voice. Page 112.

Thomas Inman (see bibliography). Page 38.

Museum of Fine Arts, Boston. Page 35.

Archive of the Institute for Sex Research, Bloomington, Ind. Page 45.

Musée du Lourve, Paris. Page 58.

British Museum. Pages 39, 67 (top), 71 (left), 71 (right).

Ronald Villeneuve (see bibliography). Pages 41, 48.

Minotaur, Paris (1933). Page 107.

The New York Times/Photo Manroe Warshaw. Page 24.

Pompeii. Photo Antonia Mulas/T.K. Rose. Pages 74, 77.

Museo Borgia, Pompeii. Page 67 (bottom).

Museo Naz, Naples. Pages 68 (bottom), 69, 76, 79.

Museo Rafael Larco, Lima, Peru/Les Editions Nagel. Geneva, Switzerland. Pages 70 (bottom), 73, 80.

Gérard Nordman. Geneva, Switzerland. Pages 84, 85, 88.

Graphische Samlung Albertina, Vienna. Page 90 (top).

Victor A. Lownes, London. Page 85, 90 (bottom), 91.

Tom Wesselman/Sidney Janis Gallery, New York. Page 96.

Museum Der Stadt Aachen, Germany. Page 83.

Germanisches Nationalmuseum, Nuremberg. Page 82.

Playboy Enterprises Collection. Page 95.

Fresco, House of the Vettii. Photo Antonia. Page 78.

Private Collection. Page 53, 89.

Museo of Pompeii. Page 76, 77.

Museo della Magallena, Lima, Peru/Les Editions' Nagel. Geneva, Switzerland. Page 70 (top).

Jean Cannelies Collection/Les Editions Nagel. Geneva, Switzerland. Page 72.

André Emmerich Gallery. New York. Page 75 (top).

Paul Margiotta/Dalia Tawil Gallery. New York. Page 94.

Ian Woodner. New York. Page 92.